How to
Organize, Create
and Produce

ADVERTISING
THAT SELLS

Today's "Magic Bullet"
for Any Business
That Needs to Advertise

DICK HILL

Hill Top Publishing
Edina, Minnesota

Dedication

To Ray Mithun, founder of Campbell-Mithun, Inc., my mentor, my favorite boss and member of the Advertising Hall of Fame.

The Book's Mission

1. To provide a valuable advertising manual for any growth minded business without an ad agency.

2. To partner with the person responsible for leading their company's communications — and help maximize their professional skills.

3. ...and importantly, to make companies more competitive by strengthening their overall marketing communications activities.

Foreward

By Robert B. Pile

Dick Hill has honored me by asking me to write a foreword for his book, which I am glad to do. I was in the advertising business for more than 40 years, and in retirement, I still am. I still write marketing plans and advertising copy for a few businesses here and there.

I love the advertising business, and I leap at the chance to write or talk about it. Advertising is a fascinating subject, and its place in a free enterprise society is critically important. Advertising is also thoroughly misunderstood by the mainstream media which leads them to publish pieces that are not only misleading and often untrue, but in many instances, downright hostile.

In spite of the complicated and often misunderstood image that advertising has, advertising itself is actually pretty simple. And the reasons for advertising, its basic objectives, are easily understood. The fundamental purpose of advertising is to *help sell a product or service*. A second purpose is to *create an impression* of a product or service to make it something the consumer wants or needs.

What makes advertising work best is a *gifted* product or service. A gifted product is its own best advertising. A gifted product makes it far easier to write good advertising in its behalf. Advertising people, therefore, should work hard to persuade their managements to innovate and make constant product improvements. Innovation in products is just as much a form of creativity as clever copy.

A product that is "me-too" makes it difficult to turn out anything but "me-too" copy. Far more often than not, advertising is asked to sell a product that at best is only as good as the competition's (and maybe not nearly as good). So if advertising people can convince their company management to spend money bettering the product—giving it some kind of exclusivity—its advertising would be far more effective.

Not many people in top management understand what I've just said here. But the good ones do, the leaders in brand market share. Proctor & Gamble (to name one) understands it, General Motors, with their Saturn form of service, understands it. Callaway Golf, with their hugely innovative clubs, clearly understands it.

Because there are lots of products today that are similar, what we are seeing is lots of advertising that desperately tries to be different. And rather than making the product different, advertising itself becomes not the means to an end, but the end itself. And the advertising industry is feeding this cockeyed premise with programs of annual awards. And the people who judge the advertising base their vote entirely on the look and sound of the ad without having a clue as to whether the ad worked or not.

I think this is pretty sad and pretty silly.

Now then, about Dick Hill's book that couldn't be timelier. Dick's objective is to perform a major-league service to someone in the job of being the communications force in a medium-to-small business. This is a noble objective and I feel Dick has turned out a remarkable work. He serves as "your advertising agency" to provide a professional look to your work. Also, he points out cost efficiencies.

It is a useful book. It's a "how-to" manual. Just about everything you'll need to know about how to help your company spend its advertising dollars....is in this book. I'd suggest you read the book from cover to cover and then do it again. Mark certain pages and paragraphs that particularly intrigue you.

You'll find that this book becomes your friend, your assistant. Use it, believe in it. It's good stuff.

About Robert Pile

Mr. Pile has spent 40 years in the advertising business, most of those years with one of the country's ten largest advertising agencies. He has covered just about every part of the business, from managing large multi-million dollar accounts, to writing copy for a small local retail store. When he retired, he was one of two senior vice presidents in a half-billion dollar ad agency. He has written two novels about advertising and many articles for magazines and newspapers. He is still very active as a speaker around the country.

About The Author

No other advertising specialist has a similar background as Dick Hill. He has excelled on the agency, client and media side. His sales and marketing experience comes from 35 years with leading companies. Including Webb Publishing, The Farm-Oyl Company and Campbell-Mithun Advertising (now Campbell Mithun Esty), where he worked on Fortune 500 accounts as a copywriter and in account management. Accounts include: Kroger Food Stores, Northwest Airlines and American Dairy Association.

The author has won numerous creative and marketing awards. He's a member of "Who's Who World Wide" and American Seminar Leaders Association. He was decorated for his front line broadcasting in Korea, where he served as a U.S. Marine Corps Radio Correspondent.

A University of Minnesota graduate, Dick Hill majored in journalism and broadcasting. While attending school, he interned at WCCO Radio, Minneapolis, one of the nation's top stations.

During his early career in Minneapolis, Hill worked with Harry Reasoner of CBS' "60 Minutes" fame. They distinguished themselves by winning the Robert E. Sherwood TV award for their provocative documentary series, "Twin City Heartbeat." Soon after, Hill won a copy writing job with Campbell-Mithun in Chicago. Reasoner joined CBS in New York. Both had banner careers in their respective fields.

The author lives in Edina, Minnesota with his wife, Mary. Together they manage a marketing communications service. Their enterprise includes workshops, consulting, public relations and special projects.

Dick Hill Marketing Communications books are appropriate for professional development, seminars, training programs, premiums and specialized reprint activities. They can be ordered through retail outlets everywhere or by calling the publisher at (612) 941-3837.

Contents

How to organize and operate the advertising function of any business — from home-based to major operations — without the extra expense of a costly advertising agency.

Like Dr. Edward Deming's 14 famous points for re-engineering organizations, here are the author's 14 ways for strengthening your marketing communications.

Now! Function "like an ad agency" with this proven ad-making system. It'll help you perform like a "pro."

Advertising and its tools have changed. But not the basics that make people buy.

Creating advertising that creates sales is the name of the game. So, cut through the clutter by raising awareness — not budgets.

Create your own identity. Be easily recognized. Your layouts should have a consistent look. Make you stand out.

Introduction

With shrinking markets, fierce competition and declining customer loyalty, many companies face some monumental challenges. More than ever before, small to midsized organizations need to develop innovative ways

Today's marketplace...

to attack the marketplace. A good starting point is to make sure you're getting as much "bang" out of your advertising as possible. This book can help you do it.

Interestingly, only a few businesses have megabucks for mass marketing. Yet, many companies spend their budgets as if they had unlimited resources.

Example: Overpaying for graphics or printing. Ignoring advertising coop monies due them. Spending ad dollars on non-priority projects. Or watering down a promotion by over-buying too many kinds of media, vs. having *one major thrust* for more impact. Or attempting to create "clever" advertising that would be counter productive for their product or company image.

...requires innovative advertising.

It is no surprise that those innovative companies adjusting to change, or reengineering, are profiting the most in the marketplace. For one thing, they're using today's technology to work smarter and faster. For another, they're outsourcing some of their marketing communications workload that used to be done internally. And lastly, they're eliminating the waste that is often taken for granted in advertising.

With budgets tighter than ever, companies must find new ways to communicate more effectively. And that's the purpose of this book. It focuses on today's systems and technology to help individuals be more productive; organizations more competitive. Importantly, the book provides the tools to help stretch your budget, sharpen your image and strengthen your sales—*without* the extra expense of a costly advertising agency.

1

Today's Communications System

How to organize and operate the advertising function of any business — from home-based to major operations — without the extra expense of a costly advertising agency.

Good communications are vital to business success. By using today's technologies and by outsourcing special projects, *one individual* in a small to midsized company can effectively manage today's marketing communications. And all without the *extra expense* of a costly advertising agency.

Here is the range of activities that you, as the person responsible for advertising in your company, can effectively handle. Including:

- Creating advertising, sales and marketing material

- Media planning and placement

- Working with suppliers

- Developing special events and promotions

- Processing coop credits

- Initiating PR opportunities

No longer called an "advertising department," today's Communications Center provides the full spectrum of a company's communications activities. Obviously, the job function will vary with each company. In many cases, the person handling the advertising duties may have responsibilities in other areas also.

The physical size of your Communications Center is unimportant. Today it is the computer that counts as most material can be produced electronically from design through production. This eliminates manual assembly, keylines and negatives. Today's easy-to-use hardware and software is affordable. It puts you on an even playing field with larger competition. And by adding your own creative talents the results are unlimited, as you'll see from the many examples in the book.

Advertising Checklist

Here's a checklist for organizing and operating a modern, efficient Communications Center.

Chances are you already own some of the equipment and material that you'll need. Check-off what you have. (✓)

A. "Equipment:"

❏ **Desktop publishing system** - This is the heart of your operation. It'll produce most of the communications material you'll need. If you prefer, you can outsource this service.

❏ **Fax machine** - For sending P.O.'s, rough layouts and instructions. For receiving bids, costs, information and media data.

❏ **Copy machine** - With reduction and enlargement features, you can create rough ads, posters, brochures and flyers. Plus, you can produce multiple copies of material for sales people.

❏ **Answering machine** - Voice messages are an important part of doing business. Don't let your message get old and tired. Keep it fresh. Change it often. Some units are multi-purpose and include a copier, fax and answering services.

❏ **35mm or digital camera** - You can save a lot of money by shooting your own pictures. Today's cameras are fool-proof and allow you to be a good photographer.

❏ **Camcorder & VCR playback** - Video tape marketing can be used effectively at trade shows and sales meetings, for training purposes.

❏ **Cassette player** - For the many audio tapes that will cross your desk. Including, demo commercials, radio station air checks, workshop and seminar presentation tapes.

❑ **Files** - For all your advertising hard copies, records, ideas and administrative purposes.

B. "Paper-Trail & Housekeeping Tips"

❑ **Job outline (Ad-Link System)** - The author's unique Ad-Link System helps you organize, process and execute your ad project.

❑ **Purchase orders** - P.O.'s help you leave a paper-trail that is necessary in today's business world. Always carry some P.O.'s with you.

❑ **Job jackets** - There is no better system or organizer than an individual job jacket. It holds and keeps track of the myriad of data that most projects accumulate.

❑ **Production estimates** - For major projects you'll want to prepare a production estimate. It will include a list of your suppliers, costs and total estimate of your job.

❑ **Company Fact Book** - Here's a valuable tool for every company. Your fact book will include market data, advertising requirements, including, copy platform, slogan, use of logo, print run numbers, etc.

❑ **Calling cards** - Leave your mark with the media and supplier representatives you work with. Also, calling cards help promote your company while attending outside meetings, workshops, etc.

C. Supplier Network

Maintain an up-to-date file on suppliers, including:

❑ Printers

❑ Ad specialist (for copywriting and special projects)

❑ Media representatives

❑ Graphics and art services

❑ Pre-press source

❑ Premium and incentives representatives

❑ Others, as needed

Use a traditional Rolodex file or file them electronically.

D. Idea File

❏ An idea file is invaluable for possible spin-off ideas. Your resource file should include samples of good advertising, competitive ads, promotions, research, success stories and industry trends. Use a manila folder or file the data electronically. Start clipping.

Desktop Publishing

Through the magic of the personal computer, you can be on an even playing field with larger competition. You can produce sharp, attractive looking brochures, flyers, signs, sales literature, booklets and newsletters — in black or white or vibrant color. Also letterheads, policy manuals — even business cards.

Today's pre-press systems will give you a competitive edge in reaching customers. Whatever your support network — salespeople, dealers, distributors or retail outlet(s) — you'll have the tools to supply them with the important materials they need. And you'll be able to do it fast and cost effectively.

Shop your system before you buy. Ask friends what they're using. Ask about any shortcomings. You want to make sure you've got the latest model that will produce a full-range of communications' material. Take a tour of their workplace and ask for samples of their output.

Computer standards are changing rapidly. That's why it would be inappropriate to list a specific model number. For best performance, here's what you'll want:

• A fast computer

• Modem

• Large color monitor

• Scanner

• Laser printer

You can operate the system yourself or use your most computer minded person. Or, hire an intern with computer experience. They could even work for you on a project basis right on your premises.

Example of desktop publishing. This computer-created ad touts all the information bike buyers need.

You can still benefit from desktop publishing without having to own the system. There are many capable sources you can utilize. They're listed from most to least expensive:

- Desktop publishing companies

- Full service printers

- Copy centers (i.e., Kinko's)

- Free lancers ("Bedroom" publishers)

If you choose to create designs yourself, keep these six design tips in mind:

1. **Create a hierarchy.** Through the use of larger or bolder type and the use of lines and boxes, you control what is most important. The hierarchy you create helps the viewer understand how the information is organized and makes your message easier to comprehend quickly.

2. **Don't overemphasize.** Once you create a hierarchy, don't give too many things top priority. If you try to emphasize everything, you'll succeed in emphasizing nothing.

3. **Be consistent in your use of type.** There are thousands of typefaces available, but that doesn't mean you have to use them all. The best looking pieces show restraint, using only a couple of typefaces. They are also consistent from page to page and piece to piece. A good place to start would be to choose an easy to read serif typeface for body copy, and a sans-serif typeface for headlines. Try to choose typefaces in which you have several weights (i.e. light, medium and bold) to give you more flexibility while maintaining a consistent look.

4. **Emphasize important ideas with graphics.** As the saying goes, "A picture is worth a thousand words." Illustrations, charts and graphs can often communicate an idea more quickly than text. Don't make the viewer search for the message, serve them the message on a silver platter.

5. **Use white space.** Don't be tempted to fill every square inch of paper. White space makes a piece look more inviting. White space can also be used around headlines to draw even more attention to them.

6. **Don't cut too many corners.** Be careful when compromising your advertising in an attempt to save a few bucks. Cheap paper, fewer colors and slipshod printers can save you some money, but the biggest waste of money is creating something that doesn't get noticed.

Going In-House

Are you using considerable media and paying full commission rates? If you have the in-house capabilities to supply "camera ready" ads for print and broadcast, you could qualify as a full fledged in-house advertising agency. You'd then be eligible to pocket any 15% commissionable rates. Plus, you may find other benefits, including:

> *Create a new profit center.*

- Discounts when buying advertising specialties and incentives, where applied.

- The lowest rates from wholesale printers (i.e., calling cards, name stamps, etc.)

- New profit center for your organization if you offer ad services to smaller companies in your community.

Today in-house advertising agencies are common. Many larger organizations use both their own in-house agency for day-to-day advertising needs, and utilize an outside agency for special assignments. Setting up your company's in-house agency is relatively simple. First step, develop a name. (i.e., "Advertising Pipeline," per samples.) Administratively you'll need letterhead, media contracts and calling cards. That's it. Now you're in business.

Example of a successful In-House Agency that produces award winning advertising.

Sample of a multi-purpose In-House Agency contract for newspapers, shoppers, magazines, radio/TV—all media.

More Protection! Less Inventory!

Heavy-duty Line-up — Farm Oyl's premiere products represent 95% of your lubrication needs. FRONT FOUR is the way to go!

GP-3 FUEL SAVER ENGINE OIL
Single inventory, all climate protection for Diesel and Gasoline Engines. Meets Mack EO-K. Your choice: 15W-40 or 10W-30. Both API CD SF.

AG-MASTER HYDRAULIC/TRACTOR FLUID
One fluid for all equipment. Industry's most advanced formulation. Can be used for all hydrostatic applications. State-of-the-art technology.

MP GEARMASTER GEAR OIL
For all automotive and heavily loaded gear sets. Can be used in place of oils calling for GL-1 service. You'll want to put Gearmaster on your team.

MOLY PLUS GREASE
Ultra-high temperature performance and water resistant. Formulated with Extreme Pressure additives. plus Moly-Disulfide to insure long bearing life.

Save Big during Farm-Oyl's Big Drum Sale!

Sample of an In-House Agency produced ad.

Company Fact Book

A valuable tool for your Communications Center — and your entire organization — is a Company Fact Book. Preparing and maintaining one will give you a better "feel" for your company, market and industry. (And show top management that you're qualified for the communications job.)

Work on the Fact Book every day. (A few pages or a section a day.) Don't try to do it all in one swoop. And obviously, you'll need to work with other departments to compile all the information. Further, it is never done. It's an on-going marketing and executive tool. Having compiled it, it'll be useful to you when talking to management. (You'll be a more valuable person.)

Tip: If your organization doesn't have a mission statement, take the responsibility and create one. Then, share it with top management. It may be the one they approve and use.

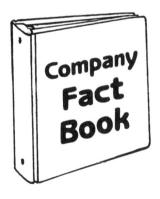

How To Build Your Company Fact Book

To do a better job on the advertising-side, know your business-side. Bound in a 3-ring notebook, your Fact Book will contain company history, product and industry information as well as advertising and sales promotion data. It's a tool you'll use every day.

I. **Company Profile**
   A. Company mission
   B. Brief history
   C. Milestones
   D. Company organization and personnel

II. **The Industry**
   A. Definition of your industry
   B. Major competition
   C. Future of your industry

III. **Product Information**
   A. Product or service definition
   B. Consumer profile
   C. Product/Service opportunities

IV. **Sales & Marketing Data**
   A. Business/Marketing plan
   B. Market share (vs. competition)
   C Customer list (or top 100 customers)
   D. Distribution opportunities

V. **Advertising & Sales Promotion**
   A. Budget
   B. Marketing supplier list
   C. Competitive ads
   D. Customer data base system
   E. Ad specifications
      1. Copy platform, theme line/slogan, copy points, etc.
      2. Use of logo
      3. Type face specs

Setting the Budget

Good news! The money for additional advertising is usually "there." But it's a matter of getting top management to transfer it over to *your* budget. There'll be times when

you need new dollars for unexpected media opportunities that pop up. Or, for firing-up a fast promotion to accelerate sales.

One of the best examples of budget comparisons is this one from my friend, Robert Pile, who wrote the foreword of this book. You may want to use it, also.

> "When discussing advertising budgets with clients, I ask them to imagine themselves in a car on the highway. If they are in the lead of several cars, all they usually must do is keep applying the same amount of gasoline to stay in the lead (this helps to keep them from cutting the budget). Or, if they are a bit behind and want to catch up, they won't do it by applying the same pressure on the gas pedal—they've got to increase. If they are at a standing start and the competition is far ahead, mere advertising pressure won't do it—they've got to make an important product change or do something dramatic to totally change the situation."

Things will go much better in budget planning if you can show management what competition is spending. These figures are not as hard to get as you'd think. They can be put together from media sources, and are worth spending some money to get.

Types of budgets you may be responsible for:

- Annual advertising budget
- Special events or campaigns
- Coop budget.
- Sales meetings
- Trade shows
- Special packaging, labels, etc.

There is no magic formula in setting budgets. Here are two of the systems I've used:

- Allocate a specific percent of your gross sales to advertising. This can range from 2-10% or more, depending on your product/service or market situation.

- Arbitrarily set a budget you can afford. But a word of caution, if the budget's dangerously low, it could be a waste of money. In today's marketplace advertising costs are considerable.

Factors to consider when setting budgets:

- Higher market share usually requires higher ad expenditures.

- New product activity requires higher ad expenditures.

- More aggressive advertising is needed for faster growing markets. (Opposed to stable or mature markets.)

- To drive more sales or increase market share, a bigger budget is required.

- Lower plant capacity typically requires higher expenditures.

- Premium priced products require higher ad expenditures.

It has been my experience that once a growth-minded company allocates monies toward an on-going advertising program, they'll become ad-budget believers. Advertising, when looked at as an investment, not an expense, can pay huge dividends.

What's Out	What's In
• Advertising Departments	• Communications Centers
• Manual layout assembly	• Desktop Publishing
• Doing everything yourself	• Outsourcing
• Company size	• Company speed
• Order taking	• Creative salesmanship
• Mass marketing	• Target marketing

Look how desktop publishing sells! Park Reupholstery generates sales leads with these distinctive 2 col. x 4 inch ads.

2

14 Ways to Strengthen Your Marketing Communications

Like Dr. Edward Deming's 14 famous points for reengineering organizations, here are the author's 14 ways for improving your marketing communications.

New times. New challenges. New direction. Today's secret for success has changed. There is less room for waste. A need to do things at the lowest possible cost and still get maximum impact. As the person responsible for communications in your organization, you'll want to use these 14 points. Make them your 14 commandments. Most of the points are covered in greater detail in following chapters.

1. **Plug-in today's digital technology.** Through the magic of the personal computer, you can help level the playing field against your major competition. Today's pre-press tools can improve your productivity and your corporate image. You can prepare eye-catching brochures, newsletters, catalog sheets, sales literature — all the support material you need to deliver more sales.

2. **Develop a marketing plan.** A good marketing plan, like a compass, can lead an organization in the right direction. In the simplest of terms it describes the process by which your business attracts and keeps customers. A meaningful 12 month plan includes:

   • Your mission statement

- Business objectives

- Sales goals

- Your marketing message

- Major sales events

- Budget and media plan

3. **Outsource special projects.** Due to leaner staffs, more and more organizations are farming out some of their marketing, advertising and PR projects. Help is abundant. As a result of corporate stream-lining, outside advertising specialists are more available than ever before. Never used one? They make valuable suppliers. For one thing, they won't waste time "re-inventing the wheel." For another, they can give you an outside perspective that can't be achieved in-house. And the best part, as the Wall Street Journal recently report-ed, the fees for a retired specialist are modest compared to the poten-tial payoff and benefits they offer.

4. **Take an image audit.** Time to take inventory. Review your commu-nications efforts annually. (Ads, brochures, sales literature, newslet-ters, P.O.P., etc.) If possible, do it with a co-worker or outside friend. Here's a checklist to follow:

- Is the material appealing?

- Is it customer oriented? (Or, too self-serving.)

- Does it contain a compelling benefit offer?

- Does it deliver a message of confidence to customers?

If you see ways to improve your communications, do it. Because for the advertiser whose budget is limited, you want every communica-tions piece to build awareness for your company. ("So-so" advertis-ing won't get the attention you need to build more sales and profits.)

5. **Develop a selling slogan.** Find your most promotable competitive edge. Then turn it into a powerful marketing message. Then use it in all your advertising — brochures, catalog sheets, newspaper ads, radio, etc. By repeating your message you'll help customers better remember your product or service. And if it's a good one, you'll "burn" it in their minds.

6. **Create advertising impact.** To get the most "bang" from a limited

An example of the "digital revolution." Hirshfield's explosive ad bypass-
es film and plates and utilizes direct-to-press printing

budget, target your media for one major thrust. Find and focus on the media mix that most effectively reaches your current and potential customers. (Direct mail and radio, for example.) "Rifle-shoot," don't "shotgun" your advertising.

7. **Be sales-driven.** Always ask for action in your ads and sales literature. Invite the reader to phone or write for literature or place an order. By including a free offer on your new product booklet, for example, your ad will generate more readership and inquiries than without an offer.

8. **Claim your coop.** Take advantage of the advertising opportunity that many manufacturers offer. On a 50/50 coop basis you double your budget.

9. **Draw on experience.** When you're stumped on a project or need feedback, reach out to your Mastermind Group for help. Draw on their expertise for direction, ideas and opinions. Networking can give you new perspectives and help improve your performance.

10. **Maintain an idea file.** Clip out and save success stories, special ads, industry trends, research — whatever applies to your business. Refer to it as needed for possible spin-off purposes. It can be kept in a simple manila folder or filed electronically.

11. **Add the impact of color.** Color improves the effectiveness of any document. Adding just one color to your letterhead will increase awareness and enhance your image and how your company is received. Use 4/color for your major marketing pieces. (i.e., Corporate image piece.)

12. **Take advantage of "free" publicity.** Every organization has a story to tell. That's why you'll want to communicate information about your people, new product or service, special events and milestones. The media welcomes newsworthy stories. So send your news release to newspapers, business publications, trade magazines, radio and TV. Outsource your PR project if necessary.

13. **Make your advertising user-oriented.** Tell prospects what you can do for them. The best advertising reaches out to the qualified prospect's problem and offers a genuine solution. Don't waste space in your ads with company "fluff" copy.

14. **Cut advertising waste.** Regardless of budget size there is waste in advertising. Here's how to tighten the spending:

• Review supplier relationships for better buys.

• Get several bids on major projects.

• Do each job right — and do it only once.

• Don't do an advertising piece if it won't meet your standards or raise the interest level of your company.

• Prepare a production estimate on jobs over $1,000 so you know exactly where the dollars are going.

WHY IS IT?

A man wakes up after sleeping
on an ADVERTISED mattress
and pulls off ADVERTISED pajamas
bathes in an ADVERTISED shower
shaves with an ADVERTISED razor
brushes his teeth
with ADVERTISED toothpaste
washes with ADVERTISED soap
puts on ADVERTISED clothes
drinks a cup
of ADVERTISED coffee
drives to work
in an ADVERTISED car
and then....
refuses to ADVERTISE
believing it doesn't pay.
Later if business is poor
he ADVERTISES it for sale.
WHY IS IT?

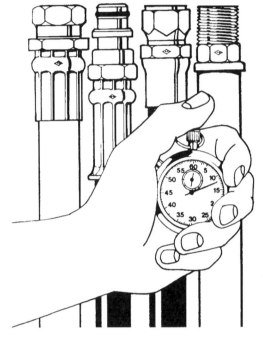

We'll replace hydraulic hose assemblies in minutes!

Rely on Ruhland's for all your hydraulic needs!

Ruhland Hardware Eden Valley — 453-2825

YOU CAN DO IT!

Simple is smart! This line art ad was easy, fast — and effective.

3

Perform Like An Advertising Agency

Now! Function "like an ad agency" with this proven ad-making system. It'll help you perform like a "pro.".

The ad-making process requires an organized system. The one I developed and continue to use is the Ad-Link System. Born out of 35 years of advertising experience, it leads you through every ad-making step. Like a "magic bullet," it'll make your job easier — and more fun. Here's the model:

Job Outline
AD★LINK SYSTEM^{SM}

Link Together to Organize, Process and Execute Your Ad Project

As you see, the system contains all the elements — from start to finish — to help organize *all* your advertising activities. All your job assignments. As you complete each step, you merely link-in the next module. The six easy-to-follow format steps "pull" the job through to conclusion. Here is how it works:

1. **Job Description** - First step, describe the project on your *Ad-Link System* job outline. It can be something as simple as "New company brochure." Then assign a number. (To be recorded on both the job jacket and job outline.) Now your job is underway.

2. **Job Menu** - Size-up your job. How important is it? How big is it? Select the appropriate power-level from the three choices below:

Job Menu Power Level (Check One)

❏ *Handsaw* - A basic, routine job

❏ *Powersaw* - A customized assignment

❏ *Laser Beam* - A major project

Make no mistake, *every* job is important. But you need to size-up your project at the beginning. This will avoid unnecessary time and money spent on minor or routine jobs. Do not over-produce or try to "re-invent" the wheel on insignificant assignments. Conversely, it is important to know when to turn on the after-burners on those projects that require extra power. (i.e., the *Laser Beam* level.) After you use this system a while, as I have, you will find it easy to evaluate your job-effort category.

> *Don't re-invent the wheel on small jobs. Put your energy where it counts.*

3. **Creative Direction** - What's the *purpose* of the ad or project? What's the *key selling idea*? The main selling points? Take time to point your job in the right direction. Write a brief description of the creative job requirements. Such as:

   "Update product catalog sheet copy. Add new features and benefits per attached fact sheet.

   Use 2/color (Red) instead of 4/color as this is an interim job until we introduce our new line next Fall."

   Or it could be several paragraphs, depending on the scope of the job. Also spell out the job specifications: i.e. layout size, number of pages, length of radio spots, etc.

4. **Budget & Administrative** - There are several ways to set budgets. First by allocating a specific amount to the project. (i.e., $2,000.) Or by first costing out the job, then setting your budget. Either way is acceptable. But be sure to keep a tight control on your money.

   Budget Tip: Allow a 10% contingency for unexpected costs.

   Regarding "Administrative," be organized and quickly follow-up on any loose-ends. Keep a "paper trail" in your job jacket. Items to file: Job outline, rough layouts, notes, costs and anything else associated with the job.

The Ad-Link System will help you raise ad-awareness. (Like this industry breakthrough ad for The Farm-Oyl Company.)

5. **Resources** - A key to successful communications is finding and "partnering" with competent suppliers. Including:

- *Ad-Specialist* - For those major projects when you are jammed internally and need outside help — and an outside perspective.

- *Desktop Publisher* - To supplement any jobs your system cannot handle; or when your internal ad center may need a helping hand.

- *Art Services* - For signs, displays or any special art or graphics.

- *Electronic Pre-Press* - Occasionally you will need negatives or stats. Most printers can line you up with this source. Or job it out themselves.

- *Printer(s)* - You may need several printers for the varied jobs you will have. From a fast copy center to a full service, 4/color printer. Most jobs, however, can be done with a small, offset 2/color printer.

- *Media* - Develop your media plan, if applicable, to the job. Then contact and meet face-to-face with the respective media reps.

- *Other Resources* - Depending on the scope of your job, other suppliers may be needed.

6. **Job Execution** - Be project-excited and each assignment will receive the attention and action it requires. Fill in the "To be done" and "Due dates" as shown on the job outline.

Here's a breakdown of the approximate percent of time required for most jobs:

- Administrative - 10%

- Creative (Preparation, copy and design) - 60%

- Pre-press (Desktop Publishing) - 20%

- Supervision (Working with suppliers) - 10%

Project Job Jackets

It is important to have a "paper trail." And there is no better system or organizer than an individual job jacket that holds and keeps track of the myriad of data that most jobs accumulate. Including:

- The job assignment (And job specs)

- Supplier(s)

- Bids and costs

- Due dates

- Job revisions

- Media schedule

- Final material

- Final costs

A standard size 10x15 manila envelope makes an ideal job jacket. Merely moisten it closed, then cut an opening at the top of the long side. If desired, you can have your job jackets imprinted.

Job Jacket for

AD★LINK SYSTEM

JOB DESCRIPTION:

JOB NUMBER:

COST:

SUPPLIERS:

REMARKS:

Keep your 'paper trail' in this 10 x 15 manila job jacket.

— Job Outline —
AD★LINK SYSTEM

Job #

Date

JOB DESCRIPTION ⟩ JOB MENU ⟩ CREATIVE DIRECTION ⟩ BUDGET & ADMINISTRATIVE ⟩ RESOURCES ⟩ EXECUTION

Link Together to Organize, Process and Execute Your Ad Project!

JOB DESCRIPTION:

JOB DESCRIPTION

JOB MENU POWER LEVEL: (check one)

JOB MENU

☐ Handsaw - A basic, routine job

☐ Powersaw - A customized assignment

☐ Laser Beam - A major project

CREATIVE DIRECTION: (Include key selling idea & main selling points)

CREATIVE DIRECTION

JOB SPECIFICATIONS: (Layout dimensions, printing instructions, script length, etc.)

(Over)

The ad-making process requires an organized system . . .

BUDGET: _____

BUDGET & ADMINISTRATIVE

ADMINISTRATIVE: Open Job Jacket to start "paper trail." File Job Outline, rough layouts, notes, costs and anything associated with job.

RESOURCES: (check one)
- ☐ In-House Only
- ☐ Suppliers Required

RESOURCES

SUPPLIERS:
- ☐ Ad Specialist _____
- ☐ Desktop Publishing _____
- ☐ Pre-press _____
- ☐ Printer(s) _____
- ☐ Art & Photo _____
- ☐ Media _____
- ☐ Other _____

EXECUTION

JOB EXECUTION: To Be Done   Due Date

1) _____   _____

2) _____   _____

3) _____   _____

4) _____   _____

5) _____   _____

6) _____   _____

. . . like this proven "Ad-Link System."

PRODUCTION ESTIMATE

- - - - - - - - - -
Date

- - - - - - - - - -
Job #

JOB DESCRIPTION: _____

_____

BUDGET: (IF ONE IS SET) $ _____

Estimated Cost:

SUPPLIERS AND WORK REQUIRED

1. _____   1. $ _____

2. _____   2. $ _____

3. _____   3. $ _____

4. _____   4. $ _____

5. _____   5. $ _____

6. _____   6. $ _____

SUB-TOTAL $ _____

10% CONTINGENCY $ _____
(10% Of Sub-Total)

ESTIMATED GRAND TOTAL $ _____

Control spending with a production estimate.

4

Fundamentals — Using the Basics

Advertising and its tools have changed. But not the basics that make people buy.

Successful advertising motivates the buyer into buying. That is why it is important to understand as much as possible about buying behavior and other advertising fundamentals.

Why Do People Buy?

Critics of advertising have said that advertising makes people buy things that they do not need. They are absolutely right. No one needs more than one pair of shoes. No one needs more than a simple shelter from the weather. No one really needs convenience foods or a different hair color. But people buy these things because they *want* them.

Conversely, advertising can't make people buy things they don't want.

> *Example:* People need transportation. In the '70's, people wanted automobiles that were economical, rather than luxurious. Result: Success of the Toyota and Honda. Death of Detroit gas-guzzlers.

Who in advertising doesn't have the scars to prove that advertising can't make people buy what they don't want? Just ask the people in Detroit who finally got the message.

People buy what they want. That's why the buyer is King! It is the *buyer*, not the seller, who determines the success of a product.

Successful Ads Motivate

How do you get people to buy your product? Basically, you motivate them. You provide them with a motive.

Motive: *Something that prompts a person to act in a certain way*

Based on the premise that people buy what they want, motivation in marketing means making people want your product. This can be accomplished in two steps:

Step 1 - Turn a need into a want.

Step 2 - Turn a general want into a specific want for your product or service.

You get people to buy your product by making them want it or you give them the product they want.

Demographics

Mention demographics and a number of characteristics come to mind:

- Age

- Sex

- Income

- Occupation

- Education

- Zip code

These demographic characteristics are valuable because they:

- Provide a broad definition of the consumer and thus the first indication of why he or she might be interested in a given product.

- Guide media selection (after the advertising has been written) so that you can maximize the number of messages falling on "fertile ground."

Buyers Are Individuals

Given two individuals with similar demographic and geographic characteristics, why does one trade cars every year while the other drives his for five-six years? Or farmers are prospects for farm equipment because farming is their business. But why does one dairy farmer have a new, high-tech dairy parlor while his neighbor uses the old stanchion system when they both have 150 cows?

The answer to both the above questions is the same because the subjects are all *individuals.* And individuals do different things for different reasons.

The 5 Levels of Customers' Needs:

1. **Physiological needs** - food, water, sex, rest, exercise, shelter. These needs have no appreciable effect on behavior except when you are deprived of them. Man does live by bread alone when there is no bread. Until these needs are satisfied, man cannot consider other needs.

2. **Safety needs** - when physiological needs have been met, man directs his attention to the next highest order.... safety needs. These include protection from danger and deprivation. Some degree of motivation.

3. **Social needs** - when physiological and safety needs have been satisfied, social needs become important motivators of behavior. These include the need for belonging, for association, for acceptance by peers, for giving and receiving love.

4. **Ego needs** - the needs of the greatest significance to man are ego needs. There are two kinds:

    • *Self-esteem* - needs for self-confidence, independence, achievement, competence, knowledge.

    • *Reputation* - needs for status, recognition, appreciation.

    These needs are rarely satisfied because once they become important to the individual, he/she seeks them indefinitely for still more satisfaction.

5. **Self-fulfillment needs** - these are the needs for realizing one's own potential, for continued self-development, for being creative in the broadest sense of the word. These needs often remain dormant because the demands to meet lower level needs require all the energy the individual possesses.

    Marketing opportunity: Concentrate on those needs that have the greatest influence on behavior and that are the most likely to be satisfied, i.e., Social and Ego needs.

    Example: Nike's make a young person feel important and confident.

Three Levels of Buyers:

- *Innovators* - They're the first to sign-up or buy. High-tech minded, they like to be the first with a new concept or product.

- *Followers* - You can get them on the "band wagon" when they see others are buying it.

- *Resisters* - Slow to buy. You've got to wait until they're ready. Nothing seems to speed up their buying process.

Create Ads That Make People Want to Buy

In his book, "How to Start And Run Your Own Retail Business," Irving Burstiner, PH.D., prepared a "laundry list" of shoppers needs and wants. Here are some of the possibilities that motivates people to buy:*

...Adventure	...Physical health
...Affection	...Popularity
...Approval	...Prestige
...Care	...Pride
...Comfort	...Profit
...Convenience	...Recognition
...Emulation	...Romance
...Esteem	...Self-fulfillment
...Excitement	...Self-gratification
...Friendship	...Self-preservation
...Fun	...Sense of achievement
...Hunger	...Status
...Love	...Thirst
...Mental health	

With respect to specific product attributes, Dr. Burstiner pointed out that shoppers are looking for such things as durability, ease of operation, economy of price, fashion, good performance, high quality and availability of service.

*Reprinted with permission. Copyright 1994. Published by Carol Publishing Group.

Brand Positioning

How do you make people want your product? One of the real secrets of successful marketing and successful advertising lies in the way a brand or company positions itself in the marketplace.

Position your brand or company:

...Against the right market

...With exclusivity

...For leadership

The most productive advertising invariably features an idea with which people can identify themselves. It enables the customer to identify himself or herself with the product advertised. Makes them feel: "That's my kind of brand — they made it with people like me in mind." Here are some examples from different beverage brands. Each has their own loyal following:

• Coca Cola

• Mountain Dew

• Surge

• Dr. Pepper

• Pepsi

When you position your product, you place it in a certain way in the consumer's mind. Here's how a brand or company is positioned:

• By the type of product offered.

• By the marketing segment for the brand.

• By the way the product is designed and packaged.

• By its name.

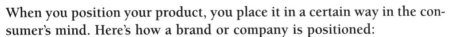

• By its price and value.

• By the system of distribution utilized for it.

• By its promotion.

One of the positioning classics that has become an advertising case study is Volkswagen. Their agency, Doyle Dane Bernbach, positioned the

Beetle as a protest against Detroit. The "Think Small" campaign made the VW a cult among non-conformists.

When it first arrived in America people stared at its funny shape. The gas station attendant had to ask where the gas goes. But as the advertising momentum built, consumers soon learned of the many benefits of owning a German Beetle. Sales went up to 500,000 cars a year. It was "advertising sizzle" at its best.

Many companies and products have been developed purposefully by the advertiser to appeal to a specific market — to people with specific needs. Examples:

- Wal-Mart

- Nike

- Healthy Choice

- Hamburger Helper

- Create a Meal

- NordicTrack

- Nordstroms

- Apple Computers

- Byerly's Food Stores

- Wonderbra

- DirecTV

- MTV Cable Television

- Chrysler's Mini-Vans

- Sports Utility Vehicles

5

Creating the Sizzle That Sells

Creating advertising that creates sales is the name of the game. So cut through the clutter by raising awareness — not budgets.

Today's advertising clutter is awesome. It is esti-mated that every man, woman and child is target-ed for over 600 messages every day. Yet, only a small percent of those ads will get noticed. And fewer will be remembered. This makes your job, as the person responsible for your company's communications, a real challenge. The key is to *raise awareness* — not budgets. By turning-up the sales-sizzle you increase the interest level of your advertising. This gives your ad a better chance to be noticed and achieve the sales you're looking for. An important starting point is to find and focus on your most promotable competitive edge.

Producing advertising that sells in not always easy. It is usually tedious. It is a demanding job to organize, create and produce advertising that changes or reinforces an attitude or behavior. Hard study, false starts and revisions are the rule. But the payoff is immense. You, as the person responsible for your company's communications, can help your organi-zation be more competitive and profitable. So study the product you are going to advertise. The more first hand information you have, the better.

Advertising Is Information

Advertising is a medium of information. Its prime purpose is to educate and inform. Yet, many treat it as entertainment or an art form. As David Ogilvy, founder of Ogilvy & Mather, said:

*"When I write an advertisement, I don't want you to tell me that you find
It 'creative.' I want you to find it so interesting that you buy the product."*

The 6 Principles of Effective Advertising:

There's a pattern to effective advertising. A direction. Principles. And the really great producers follow them. Ask these six questions before you run your next advertisement:

1. **Is there a big idea?**
   Nothing else is so important to the success of an advertisement. A genuine selling idea transcends execution. Such as the milk campaign showing Christie Brinkley and other super stars with their milk mustaches. The big idea can separate you from competition; help move people to action.

2. **Is there a theme line?**
   A theme line that presents your selling idea in a memorable set of words can generate more "bang" for your advertising. (i.e., Folger's "The best part of wakin' up is Folger's in your cup." Or, the U.S. Army's. "Be all that you can be." Or, regionally, Menard's, "Save big money at Menards.") A good theme line can give your customers a handle to hold on to — to carry your message home.

3. **Does it solve a problem?**
   People don't buy things. They buy solutions to problems. (i.e. A shovel's not for digging, but for creating a beautiful garden.) Make your advertising user-oriented. Explain clearly why your "welds" are better than the competitions. Let prospects know why your product or service is what they need — and can make life easier for them.

4. **Does the ad motivate?**
   You can neither bore, nor argue people into buying. You must persuade them with "reasons why" for buying. (i.e., features and benefits.) If possible, demonstrate your product on TV and in print.

5. **Is it exclusive?**
   The sharper the difference, the clearer the choice. You can't build demand for a product whose cardinal virtue is "sameness." Take your product out of the commodity category and make it stand out.

6. **Does it build your image?**

   The ad should enhance your product or company personality. You don't want to look shoddy or silly. And since advertising can help set you apart from a commodity image, emphasize your product, service or retail operation.

Effective advertising is not made totally by rules or guidelines. It comes from innovative people. However, I know from experience that most successful advertising has certain readily identifiable qualities, such as these six principles. Put them to work on your next ad project.

Memorable Ad Campaigns

Advertising never has to be dull. You want yours to be....noticed! Fresh! Inviting! Memorable! Here are examples of ads that were burned into people's minds. All are sales-proven, thanks to their memorable theme line, which in some cases, was also the basic selling idea. Here's ten. There could easily be 100.

- *"The best part of wakin' up is Folger's in your cup."* - Folger's Coffee.

- *"Just do it!"* - Nike Shoes

- *"The few. The proud. The U.S. Marines."* - U.S. Marine Corps

- *"Nothing beats a great pair of L'Eggs."* - L'Eggs Stockings.

- *"Betcha can't eat just one."* - Lays Potato Chips

- *"Don't leave home without it."* - American Express

- *"From the Land of Sky Blue Waters."* - Hamms Beer

- *"VISA. It's everywhere you want to be."* - VISA

- *"Some people just know how to fly."* - Northwest Airlines

- *"With A Name Like Smucker's, It Has To Be Good!"* - J.M. Smucker Co.

Memorable advertising requires exposure. And consistency. You can't keep changing it if you want to be noticed and build awareness for your campaign. Once you hit on a good selling idea, stay with it.

Copywriting Tips

Good news! Copywriting isn't the big mystery some people try to make it out to be. Not when you want your communications to be direct and reader friendly. Here are some tips to follow:

- Keep it short. (Unless an all copy type ad.)

- Get to the point.

- Use basic English.

- Talk person-to-person.

- Make it newsy.

- Build in, if you can, an emotional appeal.

- Stress one or two major selling points.

- Promise benefits.

For further help, here are some word possibilities that can help trigger a favorable reaction from readers.

The Magic Words

The right word or phrase, such as *FREE* , can build readership for your ad. Here are some of the magic words — the most *powerful words* in advertising. Keep this list handy. You'll use it often. And you'll add more as time goes by.

Free	Revolutionary
New	Easy
Sale	Fast
How to....	Event
Suddenly	Compare
Rebate	Hurry
Now	State-of-the-art
Value	High Tech
Announcing	Quick results
It's here!	Successful
Just arrived!	Proven performance
Fresh	Reliable
Guaranteed	Fun
Sensational	Marvelous
Last Chance!	Miracle
Important	Refreshing
You deserve	Achieve
Fat free	Beautiful
High quality	Love
Connect	Power
Special	System

Headlines make ads work. The best headlines appeal to people's self-interest or give news. Long headlines that say something outpull short ones that say nothing. Remember that every headline has one job. It must stop your prospects with a believable promise.

Since the purpose of advertising is to build awareness, don't hide your headline in body copy. Take a lesson from the newspapers. People choose what they read in the paper by picking headlines. Individuals read the stories that will interest them, based on the headlines. (Headlines get five times the readership of the body copy.) So, make your headline pull in your readers. Make it promise a benefit or deliver news or offer a service or tell a significant story or recognize a problem or quote a satisfied customer.

David Ogilvy, the advertising great, probably said it best regarding headlines:

"IF YOU HAVE NEWS TO DELIVER, DELIVER IT."

Headlines

"IT'S CHEVROLET WEEK AT YOUR HONDA DEALER."

I had to look twice to see who was paying for the ad. It pulled me in. And I'm sure it pulled in many Chevrolet owners as the ad offered special discounts for trade ins.

"ALL 5,000 OF OUR DEALERS HAD TO PASS A VERY TOUGH TEST. WHICH IS WHY WE DON'T HAVE 10,000"

—Lennox

"APPLE PUT THEIR BRIGHTEST ENGINEERS TO WORK IN A ROOM WITH NO WINDOWS. AND LOOK WHAT THEY DID."

—Apple Computer, Inc.

"KILLS BUGS FAST."

—Porsche Cars North America

"REDBOOK JUGGLERS. WOMEN WHO SQUEEZE THE MOST OUT OF LIFE"

—Redbook Magazine Trade Ad

"IF YOU REALLY LOVE ME, YOU'D WEAR ONE."

—Breathe Right Nasal Strips

"THISTLE FEEDERS ON THALE."

—Wild Bird Store

Headlines

TCF's free small business checking is perfect for businesses even this small.

No minimum balance. No monthly service charge. No additional relationships required. It's perfect for you. Even if your business card is bigger than your business. For details, just stop by any TCF location, or call TCF-BANK.

TCF BANK Minnesota fsb. Deposits insured to $100,000 by FDIC.

Example of how a headline can make an ad work. TCF Bank "pulls" readers in with their all copy ad.

Headlines

MAKE GOOD DOUGH. WORK FOR BRUEGGER'S

At Bruegger's, we take pride in offering the highest quality products and customer service. Our workplaces are smoke-free, grease free, clean and very friendly!

If you want to be part of a winning team that can offer lots of opportunity for advancement, a generous employee discount, and an environment that is FUN and productive, then apply today at any of Bruegger's 17 Twin Cities locations. We've got lots of opportunities cooking.

BRUEGGER'S BAGEL BAKERY®

TOTALLY COMPLETELY OBSESSED WITH FRESHNESS™

Call our Job Hot Line at 282-0228

Example of a multi-purpose headline. Besides job candidates, the ad appeals to consumers also.

Headlines

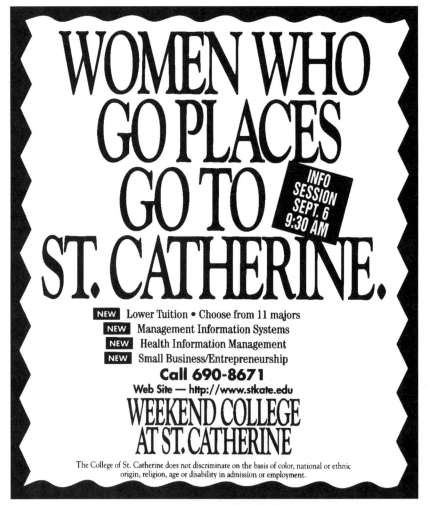

Sample of a successful recruitment series for the College of St. Catherine. Note how the headline dominates the layout.

Headlines

Statistics show that if you
grow up in Minnesota you'll be stronger,
healthier and better looking.
(Particularly if you're a tree.)

It's only natural that a state's forests should reflect the values of the people who take care of them.

Which may be why Minnesota forests are in good shape.

This according to the most comprehensive environmental impact study ever conducted on timber harvesting.

Forests cover a third of our state. Recent U.S. Forest Service inventories show 20 million trees have diameters greater than 19 inches. That's six million more large trees than existed just fifteen years ago.

The tightrope walk between our economic growth and forest management is difficult. But our state does it well—better, in fact, than other states.

We can all share the credit. Conservation interests, private landowners, governmental bodies and our forest industries are all working together to make a difference.

After all, isn't that the Minnesota way?

Since 1980, more than 243 million trees have been planted in Minnesota by public and private groups

M i n n e s o t a   F o r e s t   I n d u s t r i e s

© 1994 Minnesota Forest Industries

The Minnesota Forest Industries "plants" some good news about trees. The historic picture and headline make the ad work.

Taking the Market By Storm (Door)

Through research, Larson Manufacturing found that homeowners were rather blase about buying storm doors. That's why the Brookings, South Dakota company developed an industry breakthrough campaign. With a new marketing approach — including 4/color ads, brochures and catalogs, plus a strong dealer cooperative program — Larson Storm Doors caught the market's attention. Their campaign is raising the awareness on the importance of picking the right Larson Storm Door.

This puppy helps open the door to high readership. (Part of a 4/color magazine campaign.)

Catalog Copy Tips

Some of the best selling copy is found in catalogs. The concise headlines and copy points are a thing of beauty. And the copy sells! That's one reason the catalog business has boomed. More people than ever are buying by mail. Take some time to study their creative technique and style. Catalogs are a marvelous advertising model. Some tips to follow:

- **Headlines** - Their headlines are like an arrow to a target. No fooling around, they tell you quickly "what's for sale."

- **Body Copy** - It's some of the most meaty, crisp, tight, well written professional copy you'll find. Shoppers like the features and benefits that are showcased. Catalog writers know how to squeeze in every copypoint possible.

- **Product Photos** - Most are found in 4/color to capture the full essence of the item for sale. Most companies use photography vs. illustrations. Catalogers must have been responsible for that old, old saying: "A picture is worth a 1,000 words."

Catalog Copy Sells

"NO DESIGNER DOODADS ON OUR MESH KNIT POLO: JUST FIVE BETTER DETAILS FOR ONLY $21."

—Lands End Direct Merchants

"OUR STOWAWAY JACKET NEVER WRINKLES.

Wash it. Wear it. Sleep in it. This lightweight jacket's superfine polyester microfiber seersucker means no wrinkles. Not one, not ever."

—Norm Thompson

"SOME CURVES YOU JUST CAN'T GET FROM WORKING OUT. THE MIRACLE BRA, NOW 50% OFF."

—Victoria's Secret

"I WENT AROUND THE WORLD IN THESE SHOES!

I put them on at 7 a.m. every morning and did not get back to the hotel until 9 or 10 at night. From showroom to showroom, city after city, country after country. Easy Spirit shoes are the most comfortable shoes I've ever owned."

—Thea Iglehart
General Merchandise
Manager
Mark, Fore & Strike

"ROYAL RIVIERA® PEARS

So big and juicy, you eat them with a spoon. Available only from us, this rare and exclusive gourmet fruit remain one of the world's great eating experiences. If you've never tried them yourself, we envy you your first taste."

—Harry and David

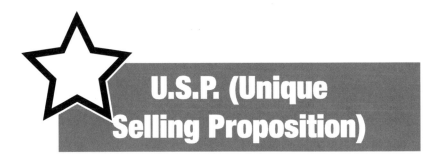

U.S.P. (Unique Selling Proposition)

"Why should I buy from you?" That's what prospects are thinking when they see your advertising. A U.S.P. (Unique Selling Proposition) statement could help strengthen your advertising; help separate you from competition. As you'll see from the examples, it differs from a slogan or theme, in that it uniquely underlines your competitive advantage.

Your Marketing Message

How do you go about developing an advertising message that best fits your company? Daniel S. Kennedy, in his book, "The Ultimate Marketing Plan," summed it up this way:

"Find your most promotable competitive edge, turn it into a powerful marketing message, and deliver it to the right prospects."

*(Reprinted with permission from The Ultimate Marketing Plan by Daniel S. Kennedy. Copyright © 1991, Daniel S. Kennedy Publishing by Adams Media Corporation.)

This concept — finding your most promotable competitive edge — is akin to the *Unique Selling Proposition* (U.S.P.) that can influence prospects to buy your product. It tells your audience that yours is a "gifted" product, not a commodity item, and shouldn't be compared with competition. Unlike a slogan or theme that most advertisers use, a U.S.P. statement is a motivating idea, uniquely associated with a particular brand, to be registered with prospects.

Here are some examples:

Advertiser	Marketing Message:
• Cub Foods	*"Low Price Leader."*
• Smucker's	*"With A Name Like Smucker's, It Has To Be Good!"*
• Kinko's Copy Centers	*"The New Way To Office."*
• Maytag	*"The Dependable People."*
• Gedney Pickles	*"The Minnesota Pickle."*
• Enterprise Car Rental	*"We'll Pick You Up."*
• John Deere	*"Nothing Runs Like A Deere."*
• National Fluid Milk Processor Promotion Board	*"Milk. Where's Your Mustache?"*
• Greyhound	*"Take the bus and leave the driving to us."*

Idea Development

Many a great idea started on a napkin during lunch. Including some of the advertising campaigns running today. But the most common thinking-tool is a legal pad. It's something I've used all my career. And I always keep it close, because you never know when an idea will strike.

But don't be too quick to expose your idea or concept to top management. Because ideas start as seeds. They need fertilizing, cultivating and nurturing. I've seen many a good idea "killed" because it was presented too soon.

Some steps to take when developing your idea:

1.   Write a rationale about your idea or concept. Keep it short and simple.

2.   Rough out any layout or example that may be needed.

3.   Get an opinion from a colleague or friend.

4.   Get "ball park" costs, if applicable.

5.   Present idea for approval.

Communications Effectiveness

Make sure your advertising gets people talking about you. That way, you generate the most effective communications there is — *word-of-mouth advertising.* In order of importance, here is the ladder of communications effectiveness:

1.   Person-to-person conversation. (Word of mouth)

2.   Meeting or group discussion.

3.   Telephone conversation.

4.   Handwritten letter.

5.   Mass produced letter.

6.   Newsletter.

7.   Brochure. (Sales literature)

8.   News item. (Press release)

9.   Paid advertising.

Knowing that word-of-mouth is the most effective type of communications, many advertisers use the person-to-person approach. It is called *slice-of-life* advertising. P&G has used this format for years, showing a friend recommending a tried and trusted product to another friend.

Here's the "slice of life" format for TV commercials:

1. We see person with pain or problem.

2. Friend or V.O. Announcer introduces solution.

3. Person has psychological "Aha;" sees light.

4. Viewer relates to the pain/problem, and realizes he or she needs product, also.

Packaging and Collateral Copy

Take time to study all the good copy that surrounds you. Crisp, tight, well written professional copy helps consumers with their buying decisions in food stores, restaurants, hardware and do-it-yourself lumber stores — and more. The good copy we're referring to is found on packaging, labels, collateral and sales-support material. Such as:

• Cereal boxes

• Microwave popcorn

• Shampoo bottles

• CD covers

• Restaurant menus

• In-store signs

Sharpen your skills by seeing how the best and the brightest in the food industry — Proctor and Gamble, General Mills, Kellogg's, Pillsbury, Kraft — handle packaging copy and in-store signage. For anyone in advertising, each visit to the supermarket is like a "half-day marketing workshop."

"NEW SENSATIONAL TASTE...
LIKE EATING A FRESH, RIPE ORANGE"

—Minute Maid Orange Juice

New Ways to Say It

When possible, try to *break the mold* when it comes to headlines or copy. The unexpected stops readers/shoppers in their tracks. Here's one example. This goes back to my boyhood and first part-time job with National Tea Food Stores in Minneapolis. I was 12 or 13. The weekly delivery truck had dropped off more Campfire brand marshmallows than ordered. Our manager didn't want to file all the paperwork that was required to return them. He asked me to make up some signs and merchandise them throughout the store. It was my first experience with copywriting and I knew it would take some imagination, as marshmallows aren't exactly the fastest selling product in a supermarket. Here was the sign I made with a speedball pen and some butcher paper.

If it fits, pertinent humor can work well in advertising. But cuteness — as contrasted to pertinent humor — is a mighty poor substitute for effective advertising.

Sample of a toll-free phone number and website inviting readers to action.

Every advertiser would love to run full-page ads. But not every budget allows it. So "hooray" for the creative advertiser who goes "small space" and makes every word count.

Here are some examples of small ads that are making it big with readers.

Small Space Ads

OUR ENGAGEMENT RINGS COST YOU NOTHING IF SHE DUMPS YOU WITHIN 60 DAYS.

At Empire Diamond, you get a 60-day money-back guarantee on GIA certified diamond rings.

You even get a 10-day free inspection.

But, most importantly, you get to save up to half on these rings. (A fine one-carat GIA certified diamond starts at only $3,000.)

Call Empire, and we'll fax or mail you the documentation on any size you want - from $1,000 to $1,000,000.

Take a chance on love, not a ring.

DIAL·A·DIAMOND℠
1·800·SAVE·HALF

EMPIRE DIAMOND
ON THE EMPIRE STATE BUILDING'S 66TH FLOOR FOR 63 YEARS

☐ · High-quality film ☐
☐   processing ☐
☐ · Fast, one-day ☐
☐   service
☐ · 4x6 glossy prints ☐
☐ · Low price ☐
☐ · Fresh film 200-24 ☐
☐   exposure $1.49 ☐

Jamestown Color Lab
Box 509
Jamestown, N.D. 58402
(800) 648-4611

TWIN CITY RADIATOR

Full Service Auto Radiator Repair

• Flush & Fill • Water Pumps
• Radiator Repair • Heater Repair
• Gas Tank Repair

American & Foreign Cars

Same Day Service! Courtesy Ride to Work!

Near Downtown Mpls.
On U of M West Bank
1821 Washington Ave. So.

340-9420

Action Verbs

To help stimulate readers to action, here are some word examples to consider:

Achieving	Influencing
Answering	Initiate
Assessing	Integration
Avoid	Investing
Building	Learn
Capitalize	Mastering
Cash-in	Maximizing
Clarify	Monitoring
Centering	Motivating
Confirming	Negotiating
Conquering	Optimize
Create	Pinpointing
Detailing	Planning
Diagnose	Probing
Expanding	Profile
Evaluating	Providing
Exposing	Rethinking
Exploring	Revealing
Facilitating	Sharpen
Focusing	Stimulate
Gaining	Tap
Grasping	Uncover
Highlighting	Understanding
Increasing	Zero in

6

Designing Layouts That Sell

Create your own identity. Be easily recognized. Layouts should have a consistent look. Make you stand out.

Creating layouts is a whole new ball game. The new age of desktop publishing eliminates manual assembly, keylines and negatives. From design through production, most material can be produced electronically. This saves you time, improves quality and lowers costs. (Ads don't have to cost a lot of money.)

Visualize Your Ad

In print advertising, the ad making process starts with a layout. Most communications people find it easiest to first prepare a rough or overview, on paper. Then, click on the computer. With very little effort, you can fine-tune your layout to exactly the point you want it. Here's how to best *visualize* and *finalize* your ad:

3 Steps to Creating An Ad

1. First, *Think* it out

2. Next, *Rough* it out

3. Then, *Lay* it out

Your copy machine can be an important tool in layouts. You can copy art, drawings, logos and items from a score of sources that illustrate your ads as they begin to take shape and form. Visualizing and "roughing" out your idea is an invaluable step in the creative process of producing anything in print, be it an ad, sales literature, flyer, poster, etc.

Computer graphic design is easier than you think. If you do not have either the equipment or the skills to do this yourself, perhaps someone else in your company is well on the way to mastering these skills within the company. If not, consider *outsourcing* — that is, going outside the company to get your layouts and pre-press material done for you.

A Word About Outsourcing

There are a multitude of very talented people out there capable of producing computer graphic design work. Programs have been developed and refined for both Mac and the other PCs. And there are many accomplished operators who know how to use them. But it is important to first ask to see the work produced by anyone you seek with or have under consideration. You can quickly ascertain if they are a good fit to your needs in this area as a source. Next, very early determine if they can take direction. That is, will they produce for you what you want? Are they flexible in helping you achieve the kinds of ads and layouts you have in mind and are they willing to adapt to your layout desires? Now you have a fit.

Create An Eye-Trap

Your layout goal is to pull in readers. That means you want layouts that are appealing and signal a benefit for readers. Every print piece — ads, flyers, brochures, booklets or posters, for example, should also have an *eye-trap*. (The element in the layout that you want the reader to focus on — and "pull" them in.)

Eye-traps — the focus of your layouts — can be many things, including:

- The headline
- A picture
- An illustration
- Your feature product
- Your logo
- Or the layout itself

HALF PRICE REUPHOLSTERY

Have us reupholster any sofa or love seat and you get any chair just **half price!** That's fabric and labor, complete.

Don't have a sofa for us right now? Then have us do one chair at our regular low price and you save 25% on the second chair. Prices vary depending on which of our **1100 fabrics** you select, so call today.

Shop our factory showroom or phone for a no-obligation **home appointment.**

822-3157 *Park* UPHOLSTERY

Showroom Hours: Mon. – Fri. 10 am to 5 pm • Sat. 10 a.m. to 1 p.m.

Serving the Entire Twin Cities from 2909 Bryant Ave. South
Family owned & Operated Since 1952

5 DAYS LEFT TO SAVE!

Example of a consistent ad format. Readers easily recognize Park Upholstery ads.

Developing Your Own Ad Format

Developing your company's ad format is an important project. How customers and prospects perceive you can affect your business. Some key things to follow for a successful look:

1.   Create your own identity.

2.   Be easily recognized.

3.   Have a consistent look.

Your Company "Look"

The right layout format is important. By having a consistent "look" to your ads, you set your company apart from others. You gain instant recognition — like the "guy in the red car." Each ad or piece of literature reinforces this recognition factor and your advertising dollars go further because your image builds as the images compound. In a sense, you break out of the pack or herd.

To develop your ad format, and achieve that consistent look, I have set forth some very simple layout ideas you may wish to consider. In the sketch below, note the placement of the logo at top. Also the recommendation of a distinctive border, consistent in all ads you produce. Also the promise/benefit headline — it's a must for immediate communication in this day and age.

Illustration #1: Bold rule or distinctive border to set your ad apart

Command attention by your offer in the headline:

- "Three Days Only!"

- "Final Week!"

- "Lowest Price of the Year!"

- "Limited Supply"

Whatever your urge to action, don't mince words. Say it boldly and loudly. An easy to implement layout might look something like this:

Illustration #2: Hurry on down, immediacy or sense of urgency

Illustration #3: Headline reversed from retail ad. (See Hirshfield's complete ad on page 17.)

If the advertising image you wish to create is not in the retail area, and your motivation is to build confidence, stability, expertise or say reliability, your approach would be much different. The use of implied or actual endorsement from satisfied users or patrons works particularly well for a service business. This can take the form of an "Authority" column you might run in trade books, local shoppers, daily-weekly-monthly periodicals where consistent appearance is part of your grand design.

How to Save Big in Cold Weather

By Your Expert

Consistency here is the key word. Familiarity with your "audience" makes an easier connection if you have a recognized authority figure to promote. This format can build the expertise you wish to impart to potential customers. The same consistency should also apply to your phone directory classified ads or use of classified space in the want ads section of your newspaper.

It is possible to go from a virtual unknown to expert status in your business. Here is how you can build and compound your advertising efforts.

Authoritative material may be interspersed with outright commercial product information in an ad of this sort. Keep in mind that a "column" format is probably a long term commitment in your advertising efforts. Building a business with personality and authority is very good business in itself. Realtors, Body Shops, Attorneys, Insurance Agents are but a few of the businesses that benefit directly from this kind of advertising.

How Do You Sign Your Name?

That, in essence, is what you must do at the end of every advertisement. Call it the "sign off," the "logo area" or bottom of the ad. It is a very important area. The bottom of the ad is where you communicate the **who**, **when** and **where** you are open for business. Every ad, insert (or preprint) or piece of literature should conclude with consistent presentation of certain information. Your logo - who you are. Your hours — when you are open consistently or your phone number hotline or special events. Your address — how to find your place of business, sometimes more than a map, often a key intersection or area of the city, such as a mall, shopping center, industrial park, the "west end" or whatever. Often credit information, bank financing or notices of bonding or state approval are also best included at the bottom of your ads. (ANYTHING IMPORTANT FOR THE CUSTOMER.)

Logo and claim line starkly presented with surround of space

Putting Your Tools to Work

You have the Fax Machine to communicate with suppliers, any of your outsources, manufacturers or outlets. Your copier can probably make both enlargements and reductions of illustrations, clip-art, drawings, layouts and anything to facilitate your "thinking" and development process of producing an ad. Your Computer Graphic Design person can scan most "clean" art, logos or illustrations into his computer storage for use now and in the future at his instant recall. Basic ad layout, once honed and refined can be easily adapted to additional ads in a series. You can communicate with your outsource person by fax and phone. In the case of having a compatible computer, the modem is a direct communication on ad development progress with someone off premises.

Some "Tricks" of the Trade to Make You A Pro:

1. **Measure twice — saw once.** Check your publications' physical dimension requirements — how wide the columns, pages, etc. — what they call "mechanical" requirements. You'll avoid costly and time-consuming redos.

2. **Know your "screens."** Things like "line screen" refer to the number of lines of dots per inch. The higher the line screen, the higher the quality and the higher the cost. Does your newspaper require 65-line, 85-line or 100-line? Muddy reproduction can be avoided by observing these requirements. Common screens include: 65 for many newsletters and coupons, 85 for most newspapers, 133 for many magazines and quality flyers, 150 for art books.

3. **Check with others**. Never hurts to ask questions. Simply running your ads by someone "legal" in the company protects you against out-of-bound claims on products, misuse of logos or trademark and copyright protection of same. In short, learn to learn the rules. If certain people within your company must "sign off" on the ads you produce, make a copy and get it initialed OK. (If it's OKed, you're OK)

4. **Invite internal company reviews.** Listen to what they say and evaluate the same. Develop a thick skin and remember that anyone can be a critic, but few can actually "do" what they suggest you do. Inputs from fellow "powers" in your company creates goodwill and often leads to legitimate good advice and criticism. A Team approach to your responsibilities can easily develop if you are willing to share both results and the objectives you are using to achieve them.

5. **Shop "price" with intelligence.** Always know your rates from publications in advance. You may be offered local rates or consistent user rates which are much lower than one-shot advertisers. Contracts, also, get lower rates. Always verify bills which can be accessed against your advertising efforts to keep your understandings and agreements in force. It's just good business.

6. **Develop a checklist.** ALL the things which you must include in an ad. Is the objective you have well accomplished in the execution of the ad? Has all detail been carefully checked for accurate illustration and price, addressees, logos etc. Has the ad met legal requirements mentioned above?

Basic Rules Apply Across The Board

Whether you are producing that necessary piece of product literature, a full-line capabilities brochure of your company's products and/or services, a radio or television commercial, a telemarketing script or even letterheads and business cards, the basic rules of inclusion apply to your company or "corporate" presentation. They're in the checklist given below.

Your Checklist:

- ❏ Who you are — logo or identity.

- ❏ Premise for advertising piece — headline offer, i.e. "Sale," benefit, implied benefit, whether it's a savings of money, time or introductory offer.

- ❏ Offers presented in descending order, that is best offer first at top and often at/in dominating position to command the most attention.

- ❏ Clear, concise presentation of offers — what you get, preferably illustrated, clear pricing, savings, your "deal."

- ❏ Sign off at bottom or ad end — again telegraphically done with your logo.

- ❏ Statement of your "Unique Selling Proposition" or company's central idea/identity. (i.e. "Where low prices are born," "Where Service Ends in your Satisfaction," "The area's most complete inventory of building supplies," etc.)

- ❏ Location — given in terms of clear, concise address, intersection, shopping mall or relationship to well-known landmarks.

- ❏ Phone number. Wisely given for service or consumer inquiries of any sort. Don't overlook a special "hotline."

- ❏ Hours, days and times you're open — convenience to the customer.

- ❏ Credit cards, availability of financing, bonded and insured information where applicable — in short, anything to facilitate the customer in being predisposed to want to do business with you *before* he/she sets foot on your premises.

- ❏ Other _____

7

Media Planning

Find and focus on the media mix that most effectively reaches your current and potential customers.

Few businesses have megabucks for mass marketing. So target your media carefully to get the most "bang" for your buck. One common mistake is spreading advertising dollars in too many directions. Find and focus on your media mix that most effectively reaches both current and potential customers. In this way, you'll create *one major thrust* for the impact you need to reach and influence your audience.

In developing your media plan, you need first to consider all the different ways you can communicate. Here are the most widely used choices.

Media Shopping List

I. Print Advertising

- *Local newspaper and shoppers* — Ideal for timely messages and establishing local presence.

- *City/regional magazines* — Usually an upscale audience with a limited reach.

- *National newspapers* — USA Today and Wall Street Journal are read mostly by male businessmen. Expensive, but effective.

- *Trade or technical magazines* — Well focused to a specific reader. (i.e. Advertising Age for marketing people.)

- *Consumer magazines* — Expensive, but consider the classifieds that offer lower-costs.

- *Enthusiast magazines* — These vertical magazines target loyal readers with specific interests. (i.e. Fishing, antiques, snowmobiling, etc.)

- *Farm magazines and newspapers* — Besides the national farm books such as Farm Journal, there are numerous state farm books and regional farm newspapers.

- *Yellow pages* — Attracts local leads.

II. **Radio** - Radio stations appeal to a select demographic group. This allows you to reach the right audience with your message. (i.e. News/Talk, rock, country, big bands, etc.)

- *Local Radio* — A favorite with local merchants and businesses of every size.

- *Network Radio* — For advertisers that want national coverage.

III. **Television**

- *Local TV* — Cost is reasonable.

- *Local Cable* — Economical; a growing audience.

- *Network TV & Cable* — Good impact; airtime and production costs are expensive. (Note: Broadcast TV is losing its share of market to Cable Television.

IV. **Outdoor Advertising**

- *Monthly, special emphasis boards* — To showcase special events.

- *Permanent boards* — For name brands or pointing out retail locations.

V. **Direct Mail**

- *Increasing in importance.* — Trends are database oriented. When possible, personalize direct mail to the reader.

VI. **Envelope stuffers**

- *Messages get a free ride;* often discarded by recipients; must be clever to work.

VII. Telemarketing

- *More and more sales* are made via the telephone. Experience will reveal the best days and times to call. Can be used by both business-to-business and consumer advertisers.

VIII. Trade Shows

- *Many advertisers view trade shows* as critical to their marketing mix. It's one time you see customers on your home turf. Consider promotional products to build traffic. Also, try to have an exciting video presentation to draw interest.

IX. Interactive Marketing (The new media)

- *Internet* — A limited but dedicated audience — and growing.

- *Kiosk* — These store displays help consumers with their buying decisions. It's a growing in-store feature that can build awareness for your brand.

- *CD-ROM* — Beginning to catch on. They're even appearing in business books (as a bonus to the buyer.)

- *Fax & E-Mail* — Both are effective in reaching select audiences.

Direct Marketing

If you can locate and identify them, your top buying customers can become a database for profit. More and more advertisers are using direct marketing on these prime customers to keep and to gain their repeat business. This is a good time to stop and review the definition of direct marketing by the Direct Mail Marketing Association:

> *"Direct Marketing is the total of activities by which products and services are offered to market segments in one or more media for informational purposes or to solicit a direct response from a present or prospective customer or contributor by mail, telephone, internet or other access."*

Using Your Database

Nearly every customer has had a phone call, letter, a handout or a FAX from a company they've done business with. It could be from a department store, a phone company, bank, florist, an airline, a credit card company or even a local car wash. The purpose is to ask for a repeat order. Or, to announce a special customer appreciation offer. The solicitor is using their database to retain customer loyalty — and to build sales.

Every business has a customer database of some kind. An effective one should contain information about a customer's...

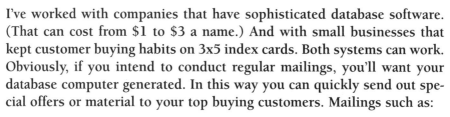

• Past purchases

• Demographics

• Buying behavior

I've worked with companies that have sophisticated database software. (That can cost from $1 to $3 a name.) And with small businesses that kept customer buying habits on 3x5 index cards. Both systems can work. Obviously, if you intend to conduct regular mailings, you'll want your database computer generated. In this way you can quickly send out special offers or material to your top buying customers. Mailings such as:

• Catalogs

• Newsletters

• Club news

• Seasonal offers

• Special announcements

• Price reductions

• New product introduction

It's important to cultivate long-term relationships with customers. Loyal customers need to be contacted frequently. And to be notified of special buying opportunities. Any database takes commitment to maintain. Updating lists is essential. This can cost $1 a name. It has been said that smart companies don't pinch pennies — they focus on customers.

Direct Mail Format

The sky's the limit regarding the format for direct mail. But the basic format for most companies is relatively simple:

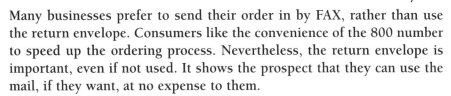

- Mailing envelope

- Cover letter

- Flyer/circular/sell sheet

- Order form

- Return envelope/FAX #/800 #

Many businesses prefer to send their order in by FAX, rather than use the return envelope. Consumers like the convenience of the 800 number to speed up the ordering process. Nevertheless, the return envelope is important, even if not used. It shows the prospect that they can use the mail, if they want, at no expense to them.

Copywriting Formulas

The late Frank Egner, one of the top copywriters of all time, listed nine tips for effective direct marketing results:

1. Write a lead to create desire as well as get attention.

2. Give an inspirational beginning.

3. Give a clear definition of the product.

4. Tell a success story about the use of the product.

5. Include testimonials and endorsements from satisfied customers.

6. List the special features of the product.

7. Make a statement of the value to the purchaser.

8. Devise an action closer that will make the reader want to buy immediately.

9. Conclude with a **P.S.** rephrasing the headline or opening.

Bob Stone, a legend in direct mail advertising, has a seven step formula that is still being used:

1. Promise a benefit in your headline or first paragraph.

2. Immediately enlarge on your most important benefit.

3. Tell the reader specifically what he or she will get.

4. Back up your statements with proof and endorsements.

5. Tell the reader what will be lost by not acting. (Pain)

6. Rephrase your prominent benefits in the closing offer.

7. Incite action now.

Where the Money Goes...Media & Methods
(1995 Statistics, in $ millions)

Daily Newspapers	36,317
Direct Mail	32,866
Television	32,720
Premiums/Incentives	20,800
Trade Shows	16,500*
Point of Purchase Display	12,024
Radio	11,338
Yellow Pages	10,236
Consumer Magazines	8,580
Promotional Products	8,037**
Coupons	6,950
Event Marketing	4,700
Business/Farm Magazines	3,842
Cable TV	3,526
Outdoor	1,263
Sampling	774
Internet Marketing	720
Telemarketing	445***

* 1996 Estimate
** Ad specialty and premium sales by distributors
*** 800 and 900-number marketing

8

Turn-Up Your Radio

Radio is a remarkably personal way to get to the minds of people. Make it a part of any major promotion you run.

It's *"hot!"* Advertisers of every kind are benefiting from the full value of radio. Its promotional power is awesome. That's why radio should be part of any major promotion you break. It works well with direct mail and newspaper. A favorite with local merchants and businesses of every size, radio's benefits keep growing.

Why Radio Is "Hot"

...Radio is fast!

...Radio is flexible!

...Radio is words *and* music!

...Radio is prices — and personality!

...Radio targets *your* audience!

...Radio can saturate!

...Radio can motivate!

...Radio can persuade!

...Radio can sell!

...Radio produces results!

...Radio is a bargain!

Radio is a remarkably personal way to get to the minds of people. It can influence. Help persuade. Help produce the sales you're looking for. You want it to be part of any major promotion you break.

Who listens to radio? Your customers do. And your competition's customers. And the prospective customers that can't make up their minds to buy your product/service, shop your store — or the other guy's. And because of the diversity of programming that radio offers, you talk to the people you need to, not the people you don't. From big band to big rock stars — or, to all talk, there's a station that will fit your product. Radio can help keep your loyal customers. Help create new customers. Help expand your market. Help grow your business.

Radio Sells Everything

Regardless of your company size or product line, chances are radio can work for you. It fits *every* business. And if you're in retail, it can deliver customers right to your door. Here's a list of businesses and product categories that are experiencing good success on radio. Bet your product or service is included.

Products/Services Advertised On Radio

- Ag Products (Seed, Feed, Machinery, etc.)

- Automobiles, Mini-Vans, Sports Utility Vehicles, Trucks

- Automotive After Market Parts & Services

- Brewers, Distributors of Alcoholic Beverages

- Boating: Boats, Equipment & Services

- Books & Learning Supplies

- Casinos

- Catalog Services

- Clothing

- Communications Products & Services

- Computers & Software

- Construction: New Homes, Home Repair, Windows, Siding

- Dairy Products

- Day Care

- Discount & Department Stores

- Drug Stores

- Education: Schools, Seminars

- Electronics

- Employment Services

- Entertainment & Sporting Events

- Expositions & Special Events

- Eye Care Services

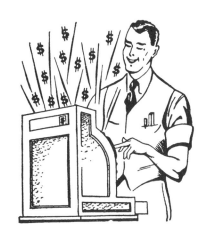

- Financial: Banks, S&Ls, Credit Unions, Financial Advisors, Stock Brokers

- Florists, Floral Delivery, Nurseries

- Food: Food Stores, Food Products, Beverages

- Freight & Delivery

- Furniture & Bedding

- Hair Care

- Hardware & Do-It-Yourself Supply Lumber Stores

- Health Care: Hospitals, Clinics, Nursing Homes

- Health Products & Services

- Heating, Air Conditioning & Duct Cleaning

- Insurance

- Janitorial Supplies & Services

- Jewelry

- Lawn & Garden

- Office Products & Services

- Outdoor Power Equipment

- Petroleum Products: Gasoline, Lubricants, Antifreeze, Fuel Treatments

- Pets & Pet Supplies

- Plumbing, Soft Water Conditioners & Related

- Professional Services: Attorneys, Consultants, CPA's, Tax Service

- Real Estate Services

- Recreational Equipment & Services: Bicycles, Snowmobiles, Personal Water Craft, Trailers, Motor Homes, RV's

- Rental Equipment

- Restaurants, Fast Food, Pizza Delivery

- Retail Shops & Businesses

- Shopping Centers & Malls

- Telephone & Supplies

- Theft Systems

- Travel: Air, Cruise, Travel Agencies, Bus Lines, Limos

- Utilities: Electric, Gas, Telephone

Top Tips for Maximizing Radio

Whether you're a long time radio advertiser or considering it for the first time, here are some proven ways that will help strengthen your broadcast efforts. Importantly, you'll find some money-saving ideas to help you get more "bang" for your radio buck.

1. **Select the right station(s).** Today's radio stations appeal to a select demographic group. This allows you to reach the right audience with your message. It could be either an AM or FM station; an all talk, country music, a hard rock or an easy listening station that best fits your product or service. Or, a combination. If you're unsure which one to use, call several stations and request a sales presentation. Ask about audience profile, coverage, rates, and key advertisers currently on the station. You'll find radio people most accommodating and easy to do business with.

2. **Run the right length spots.** If you've got a lot to say — or it's a production spot with music or a jingle — schedule :60's. But remember that full minute commercials, unless really needed, may be too long. (Especially when they're all talk.) In today's fast paced world, :30's may be a better choice. Some stations also offer "quickies" — usual-

ly :07 to :10 — that make good reminder or teaser spots for your special events. In summary, *it's the message* that determines the length of your commercials. You may end up with a combination of :60's *and* :30's that may work best for your campaign.

3. **Use music/voices to enhance your message.** If budget permits, consider a studio produced commercial, and/or musical jingle. Signature music quickly identifies you with listeners. Music can set a mood. Be more memorable. Stir emotions. Help motivate people to buy. To make your special commercial cost-effective, you'll need to get full use out of it. Many advertisers utilize their jingles for years. (It's a good way to get your message across, even if *you* get tired of it.) Before the session starts, ask for a "buy-out" on talent vs. paying reuse fees every 13 weeks. Your radio station can suggest sources for producing your commercial.

4. **Sharpen your script.** First draft radio commercials are usually stiff and redundant. Stations have the expertise to help you write crisp, memorable copy. If needed, your station can also add "canned music," voices and sound effects to make your commercial stand out from the crowd. Often the difference between an ordinary all-talk commercial — and something special — is just a little imagination. Sharpen your script for more awareness — and sales.

5. **Buy the right radio package.** There are several ways to "buy radio." Here are the traditional buys, from least to most expensive:

    A. *Promotional spot packages.* Most stations offer special commercial packages. They can range from 10-30 spots or more. The station schedules where and when your commercials will run. This is a good way for first time radio advertisers to get started.

    B. *R.O.S. (Run-of-schedule.)* Again, the station schedules when your spots will run. But unlike the spot package, you're not tied to a "package contract." You can run less spots, if you like.

    C. *Fixed positions.* Depending on availability, you can buy the time slots you want. This assures you of reaching the most listeners during that time period. For example, the 6:59 AM time slot, preceding the morning news, is a prime time for advertisers on most stations.

D. *Program sponsorship.* Many advertisers like to tie-in with news, weather, sports or special events. Besides the commercials — which can be either :30's or :60's, per the station's format — your company will also receive "billboards" that further promotes your company. Program sponsorship is an effective way to showcase your business.

6. **Pick the right voice.** Who do you want to deliver your commercial? If it runs "live" on the station, it will be read by whoever is on duty. (Unless the station pre-records it, as many do.) For a small talent fee, you may want to use a personality on the station or a free-lance announcer. Or, a regional or national spokesman. Surprisingly, the talent cost may not be all that much to use a recognizable voice. Again, consult with your station to help you find the right voice for your commercials.

7. **Promote your "experts."** If applicable, personalize your commercials with company personnel. They're the experts. It can be the owner who delivers the commercial. (If he/she is believable and has a fairly good voice.) Or, include the names of store people. (i.e., "See the pro's — Joan or John — in the paint department during our big sale.")

8. **Request promotional support.** Ask your station(s) for support to help kick-off your radio campaign. It could be a letter to your sales-people or dealers. (On the station's letterhead, of course.) Or, per-haps it's a station poster for your customers that promotes your radio campaign. Stations are merchandising -minded and can create a pro-motion tie-in for you.

9. **Hold a remote broadcast.** Today's technology is making on-site broadcasts a whole lot easier — and cheaper. So for that new store opening or open-house, go with a live broadcast from your premises. It'll build more immediacy — and excitement. A broadcast remote tells listeners that something "special" is happening — *right now.* (Which they may want to be a part of.) Car dealers have been doing it successfully for years.

10. **Testimonials.** Many advertisers have success with testimonials in their radio commercials. They can add believability and interest in your message. Voices can help animate and influence listeners to take action. The various types to consider:

   • Loyal customers

   • Well known personality

   • Simulated users (Actors)

A Wide Window of Listeners

Radio gives you a wide window for reaching your audience. It has strong listenership from 6:00 AM to 6:00 PM. (Television excels from 7-11 PM.) If you don't mind your commercials running after 6:00 PM, you can often get some terrific buys. Most advertisers, however, prefer earlier times. Agri-marketers, for example, schedule most of their feed, seed and machinery commercials between 5:00 AM - Noon. Your station will be happy to work with you in achieving the right time slots or package, for your promotion. Be sure to ask for the CPM (Cost per thousand) and the latest ratings the station may subscribe to.

Minneapolis-St. Paul AM Radio Stations

690	**KTCJ**	Adult contemporary	1330	**WMNN**	News/information
740	**WMIN**	Oldies	1440	**KDIZ**	Disney kids
830	**WCCO**	News/talk/sports	1400	**KLBB**	Big band/nostalgia
980	**KEGE**	Alternative	1460	**KDWA**	Oldies
1130	**KFAN**	Sports	1500	**KSTP**	Talk
1220	**WIMN**	Nostalgia	1590	**WIXK**	Country
1280	**WWTC**	Children's			

"Put radio in your media mix," advises Dave Lee, morning drive announcer on WCCO. "It's a remarkably personal way to get to the minds of people."

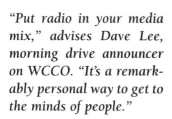

Minneapolis-St. Paul FM Radio Stations

89.9	**KMOJ**	Black comm/news/music
90.3	**KFAI**	Talk/eclectic music
91.1	**KNOW**	News/information
92.5	**KQRS**	Rock
93.7	**KEGE**	Alternative
94.5	**KSTP**	Contemporary
97.1	**KTCZ**	Progressive rock
99.5	**KSJN**	Classical
100.3	**WBOB**	Hard rock
101.3	**KDWB**	Pop
102.1	**KEEY**	Country
102.9	**WLTE**	Easy listening
104.1	**KMJZ**	Jazz
105.1	**KXXP**	Hard rock
106.7	**KFAI**	Talk/eclectic music
107.1	**WIXK**	Country
107.9	**KQQL**	Oldies

Hometown Radio

Rural, or Hometown Radio, is an important buy for many advertisers. Including:

- Local or "main street" merchants
- Agrimarketers
- Distributors
- Manufacturers

Advertisers allocate a large part of their coop budgets to rural markets.

Station Profile

WCCO Radio has been Number One since 1924.

Minnesota's
Good Neighbor

WCCO Radio 8•3•0
625 Second Avenue South
Minneapolis, MN 55402
Phone: (612) 370-0611
FAX: (612) 370-0666

WCCO's Format:
WCCO is the region's first source for news, weather and entertaining personalities.

Power and Frequency:
AM Stereo, 50,000 watts, 1-A Clear Channel, 830 kHz.

Coverage:
88 counties, including 12 which comprise the Twin Cities metropolitan area, and 76 non-metro counties in Minnesota, Wisconsin, Iowa and South Dakota.

Programming Elements:
News: Laura Dixon, Eric Eskola, Steve Murphy, Bruce Hagevik, Telly Mamayek and **Jeff McKinney** comprise the largest and most credible news team in Minnesota radio. With two daily half-hour newsblocks, complete news reports at the top and bottom of every hour and national news from CBS, WCCO is where Minnesotans tune for the latest updates.

Weather: WCCO is Minnesota's only radio station with a full-time meteorology department. WCCO is also the first source for weather-related school and business closings.

Entertaining Personalities: WCCO features the region's top personalities, including **Dave Lee,** Moose Miller, Roger Erickson, Charlie Boone, Ruth Koscielak, Tim Russell, Dark Star, Denny Long and Sue Zelickson.

Sports: WCCO is the radio home of the **Minnesota Twins,** the **Minnesota Vikings** and the **University of Minnesota football and basketball Gophers.** WCCO is also the home of the region's most listened-to sports reports and sports broadcasters including **Sid Hartman, Dave Mona, Dark Star, Herb Carneal, John Gordon, Ray Christensen** and **Paul Flatley.**

Agribusiness: Roger Strom keeps the region up-to-date on all the agribusiness news and developments, including the latest market reports.

Traffic Reports: Dean Spratt and WCCO Traffic keep WCCO listeners up to-the-minute on Twin Cities traffic and road conditions.

Example of a radio station profile to help you make your buying decision.

Radio
Success Stories

From pickles to the University of Minnesota come examples of success-ful radio campaigns. Despite product differences and budgets, there is a common tread that makes them stand out:

- Creative break-through in their copy approach.

- Consistency in carrying out the theme idea.

- Frequency of commercials. (To build awareness.)

Radio Success Stories

CLIENT: GEDNEY COMPANY

LENGTH: :60

TITLE: PICKLE PICK-UPS (MINNESOTA VERSION)

<u>MUSIC OPEN, THEN MALE VOICE:</u> Move over, lettuce and carrots. Now, Gedney's in the produce section.

<u>MUSIC AND SING: GEDNEY, THE MINNESOTA PICKLE, IS THE CRUNCHY ONE, PICKED BY HAND. ONE BITE AND YOU'LL TASTE THE DIFFERENCE. GEDNEY, THE PICKLE FOR PICKLE FANS. THE CRISPY, CRUNCHY, TOTALLY MUNCHY, HAND PICKED PICKLE FROM GEDNEY.</u>

<u>WOMAN ANNOUNCER:</u> Have you heard? Gedney's Baby Dills have gone portable in Gedney's new Pickle Pick-ups. These handy little pouches keep our pickles super-crunchy with no loose juice. Want a crunch at lunch? Pack Gedney Pickle Pick-ups. Can't take the jar in the car? Bring Gedney Pickle Pick-ups. On the run or just for fun, Gedney Pickle Pick-ups go anywhere. For fresh, crunchy pickles packed in portable pouches, pick-up Gedney Pickle Pick-ups. Pickle Pick-ups, kept crispy cold and crunchy fresh in the produce section.

<u>SING CLOSE: THE CRISPY, CRUNCHY, TOTALLY MUNCHY HAND-PICKED PICKLE FROM GEDNEY.</u>

<u>MUSIC STING</u>.

Radio Success Stories

CLIENT: UNIVERSITY OF MINNESOTA

LENGTH: :60

TITLE: "NO MORE LINES" - DAVE MONA

ANNOUNCER (OVER MUSIC): Dave Mona, public relations exec-utive — and graduate of the University of Minnesota, remem-bers when ...

DAVE MONA: I can vividly remember sitting on the steps of Northrup Auditorium and looking down the mall. It was time to register for my senior year and the leaves were turning and we were pumped up for the football opener. It was probably some-body like USC, and then all of a sudden I realized that all my days on campus were coming to an end. And it was like — hey, wait a minute. Where did all the time go? And then I remem-bered. Most of it was spent in line, registering for classes.

MUSIC EFFECT AND GIRL: Waiting in line to register — no way! Not any more.

ANNOUNCER: University of Minnesota junior, Kiaora Bohlool.

KIAORA: Today, I just register on-line. Right from my dorm room, if I want. No more registration hassles. And no more lesson in perseverance. (LAUGHS) Okay, so life at the leading edge has its drawbacks.

ANNOUNCER: In the fall of 1996, more than half of the students registering on the Twin Cities campus, registered by computer. This message has been brought to you by the friends of the University of Minnesota. The new University of Minnesota.

MUSIC STING:

That was then...  *This is now!*

Celebrating the new University of Minnesota

Radio Success Stories

CLIENT: OLD HOME

LENGTH: :60

TITLE: DRIVER/COTTAGE CHEESE

MUSIC OPEN AND UNDER FOR:

DRIVER: Most people don't think about cottage cheese, much.

SING UP FULL: FRESHEST PLACE IN THE DAIRY CASE — OLD HOME.

DRIVER: I deliver for OLD HOME ... so fresh cottage cheese is the heart of my business.

WOMAN: Meet Roger Johnson. He drives a big yellow truck for OLD HOME ... delivering famous Old Home cottage cheese ... direct from St. Paul to your supermarket.

SING: THE FRESHEST PLACE IN THE DAIRY CASE — OLD HOME ...

DRIVER: You'd think the other guys would care enough to deliver the cottage cheese direct, but they don't.

SING: THE FRESHEST PLACE IN THE DAIRY CASE — OLD HOME ...

WOMAN: That's why you should always look for OLD HOME COTTAGE CHEESE. It's creamier, tastier, fresher, because of route sales drivers like Roger O. Johnson.

SING UP AND UNDER FOR:

WOMAN: So, honk if you see a big OLD HOME truck.

DRIVER: Honk three times if you ride a Harley, OK?

SOUND OF HORN. (18 WHEELER HONKS 3 TIMES)

The Freshest Place in the Dairy Case!

Radio Success Stories

CLIENT: CUB FOODS

LENGTH: :60

TITLE: ELK RIVER "GRAND OPENING"

<u>A LA MUSIC MAN</u>

<u>LEAD:</u> You gotta' mighty good life, Elk River.

<u>CHORUS:</u> (CHANT) Good life, good life, good life. (UNDER)

<u>LEAD:</u> You're away from the maddening crowd in a great town on a clean stretch of the mighty Mississippi.

<u>CHORUS:</u> Good life, good life, good life.

<u>LEAD:</u> But . . . you've got troubles.

<u>CHORUS:</u> Trouble, trouble, trouble.

<u>LEAD:</u> Right here in Elk River.

<u>CHORUS:</u> Right here in Elk River.

<u>LEAD:</u> You're paying way, way too much for groceries.

<u>CHORUS:</u> Trouble, trouble, trouble. . .

<u>LEAD:</u> But, y'see trouble starts with T and that rhymes with C and that stands for the answer - Cub Foods.

<u>CHORUS:</u> Cub Foods. Cub, Cub, Cub (UNDER)

<u>LEAD:</u> Cub Foods is coming right here to Elk River.

<u>CHORUS:</u> Cub Foods in Elk River.

<u>LEAD:</u> And now, you're going to spend less and get more from what just may be the finest supermarket in America . . . Cub Foods. We're talking savings, oh yeah. This <u>is</u> the good life, Elk River.

<u>CHORUS:</u> We've got Cub Foods right here in Elk River. Not paying too much for groceries anymore.

<u>LEAD:</u> Opening June 5th in Elk River Center.

<u>CHORUS:</u> The good life in Elk River just got better.

Radio Teasers

Here's a "special assignment" that radio can do like no other media. That's because radio is fast! Flexible! Radio is a remarkably personal way to get to the minds of people. These are teasers — designed to set-up the launching of mailers; heat up the boiler behind your major promotion. The purpose is to call attention to "something special coming in the mail. Watch for it." Unlike small space ads in the newspaper, these won't get lost. Especially if you run a potful of them to saturate the market. Here are two suggested ten second quickies:

MALE VOICE: Knock knock.

FEMALE VOICE: Who's there?

MALE VOICE: Sir!

FEMALE VOICE: Sir, who?

MALE VOICE: Sur-prise coming in the mail from (YOUR COMPANY). Watch for it.

MUSIC STINGER:

MALE VOICE: Knock knock.

FEMALE VOICE: Who's there?

MALE VOICE: Ida.

FEMALE VOICE: Ida who?

MALE VOICE: I - da know about you, but I'm waiting for my mail from (YOUR COMPANY). It's coming. Watch for it.

MUSIC STINGER:

Sela Roofing successfully sells with yardsigns. Most of its sales leads come from this basic form of advertising.

Strengthen your layouts with special type effects.

9

10 Costly Marketing Mistakes (That many small businesses make)

Constructive criticism is productive. So check-out and avoid or correct any mistakes that you may be making.

Successful companies follow this winning formula for success: Build on your strengths — and address any deficiencies you may find. A good starting point is your marketing communications. Here are ten common — and costly — mistakes that many small businesses make. Review them to see if your company is included.

Marketing Mistake #1

Doing everything yourself. It's a noble gesture, but it's not always the smartest thing to do. Many companies sincerely believe that with a limited advertising budget they're required to do everything themselves.

Including all their communications. (From layout to the finished piece.) There may be times when it is more efficient to have some "special pieces" farmed out. Such as a special company brochure. Newsletter. Break-through ads. 15th Anniversary Sale, etc. A fresh, outside perspective can help you produce more sales. Look into it.

Marketing Mistake #2

No written marketing/business plan. There's hardly a motorist alive that would travel cross-country without a road map. With it, you make your journey easier, faster and more economical. Yet, when it comes to running a business, not every CEO or owner draws-up *their* "road map." A good marketing plan, like a map can lead an organization in the right direction. (And avoid unnecessary wrong turns.) It's the process by which your business attracts and keeps customers. It should include:

- Mission statement
- Marketing message (or theme)
- Business objectives
- Sales goals
- Major sales events
- Budgets
- Media plan

If this is your first time to write a marketing plan, check out the many software packages that are offered. Or spend some time in your local library. Or talk to other businesses and see how they constructed theirs.

Marketing Mistake #3

Afraid to change. One factor holding many companies back is the inability to try a new direction. It could be in sales, distribution, customer service, a corporate "facelift," or a new advertising look. The old saying, "If things ain't broke why fix them?" doesn't apply in today's highly competitive marketplace. (It's rough out there!) Your company could be "left in the dust" if you ignore trends taking place in your industry, for example. Many companies that I worked with were hesitant to even try different radio stations. (Even when I showed them the logic and numbers that would make the change more cost efficient.) Change is never easy. It requires a decision that many people are unwilling to make. Wilson Learning, one of the nation's top training organizations, puts it bluntly. In one of their seminars that I attended, they recommended:

> *"Lay new track or die."* (Especially if you're a retailer and Wal-Mart is coming to your town.)

Marketing Mistake #4

Shotgunning your media budget. Only a few mass marketers with megabucks have the luxury of using all forms of media at the same time. Mass media is "dead" for most advertisers. Today, it's "niche marketing." Limited budgets call for *one major thrust* when launching a promotion. It could be direct mail and radio, for example. Or radio and newspaper. By "rifle shooting," you hit the target with more impact for more awareness. So don't water down the dollars. Get more "bang" for your media buck by concentrating it on the audience you want to sell.

Marketing Mistake #5

Resisting new technology. In almost every new wave of technology, including desktop publishing and the Internet, there are those people who resist the change. (Remember the retailers slow to get in on the UPC — Universal Product Code —that's read by check-out scanners?) Many businesses wait on the side-lines too long before "getting into the game" of new technology. Where would you position your company when it comes to new trends:

- An innovator?
- Follower?
- Resister?

Marketing Mistake #6

Under-budgeted. Many advertising efforts fail for the same reason that many small businesses do — they're under capitalized. To successfully fire-up a major advertising event, for example, you need an adequate budget. By holding back dollars you can weaken your campaign to the point that it may never get off the ground. Or worse, it could look "flimsy," and uninviting to the consumer. You're better off waiting until you can allocate enough dollars to do it right, vs. going half-way.

> *Example:* A client I was working with asked my opinion of a radio jingle a friend had produced for his company. It was bad. For one thing, it had been recorded in a basement and sounded "tinny." I played some commercials that I had with me to demonstrate the need to do them professionally. My client got the message.

"Mine's pretty bad, isn't it." (He had tried to save dollars, and ended up with "nothing.") Good radio production needs to be recorded in the right studio. Anything else falls short.

Marketing Mistake #7

No clear reason to buy your product. Advertisers need to tell prospects that they have a "gifted" product or service. So to help you stand out from competition, find your most promotable competitive edge. Then, turn it into a memorable marketing message. By sharpening the difference, you give consumers (and trade) a clearer choice of your product/service.

It is important to position your product in such a way that you take it out of the commodity category. Ways to do this...

- Dig for features/benefits that "out-guns" competition.

- Develop a unique promise in your slogan.

- Create a distinctive look for your ads.

Marketing Mistake #8

Lack of company spirit and drive. Besides financial resources, it takes individuals to back a company's basic philosophy, spirit and drive. Businesses — like sales people — sometimes need to be "re-inspired." (Customers are quick to detect an uninspired employee.) As the communications leader in your organization, you'll want to set up some kind of motivation (teamwork) program. Ways to build espirit de corps:

- Make everyone feel wanted and needed through meetings.

- Develop enthusiasm and teamwork through follow-up memos and newsletters. (Keep everyone informed.)

- Launch a company-wide incentive program. (i.e., caps, T-shirts, beverage mugs, etc. with company slogan - "We're Breaking Away!")

espirit de corps - *"The common spirit existing in the members of a group and inspiring enthusiasm, devotion and jealous regard for the honor of the group."*

Remarks: No one does it better than the U.S. Marine Corps. Marines are "trained" to stay motivated. One reason is their rich tradition. By merely hearing about the flag raising on Iwo Jima or standing attention to the Marine Corps Hymn, Marines are "ready to fight." Inspire your company to action by reminding them of *your* tradition. Focus on the quality service you provide customers. Remind everyone why you're in business. It's important to keep "the juices" flowing.

Marketing Mistake #9

Missed marketing opportunities. Every organization has anniversaries, new products or services, special events, future plans, etc. Yet, these "happenings" are often under-played. Or worse, ignored. (Ouch!) Check-out your promotional possibilities. Then, roll-out your "marketing opportunity" to build more awareness for your business.

Marketing Mistake #10

Allowing advertising waste. Those companies that reengineered or streamlined, discovered a remarkable thing. Forced to down-size, they cut advertising waste they didn't know existed. (They went from mass marketing to "niche marketing" and were more careful with budgets.) Here are some of the areas to watch:

- Overpaying for graphics or printing.

- Ignoring coop monies due your company.

- Spending ad dollars on non-priority projects.

- Watering down a promotion by over-buying too many kinds of media vs. having one major thrust for more impact.

- Satisfied with mediocre marketing resources to produce your communications. (And not getting maximum awareness from your advertising.)

You should only clean your duct work if you want to be healthier!

No matter how old your home is, you could be living with dangerous indoor air! Recent studies have shown that the air in most homes is up to 100 times more polluted than the air outdoors! Pollen, mold spores, bacteria and living microbial beings of all kinds **build up in your duct work** and can cause respiratory problems, coughing, sneezing, itchy eyes, allergies and fatigue. Our approved duct cleaning process can make the air you breathe in your home safe, clean and mountain fresh. Call us now and breathe your way to better health™!

Sedgwick

HEATING & AIR CONDITIONING CO.

Comfort you can count on

881-9000
©1994 CSG

*Not all ads need photos,
as this example illustrates.*

10

Creating Effective Dealer Ads

Dealer advertising helps trigger the buying process. It tells prospects where to buy the products they need.

Manufacturers devote a lot of money and effort turning-up brand awareness. It's only smart business for independent dealers and distributors to tie-in with their own local advertising. Besides promoting your business, your ad lends local impact to the manufacturer's message or ad campaign. You're telling the customer that you are "headquarters" for the featured product. This helps trigger the buying process.

Local advertising can benefit *every* type of dealer, including:

• Appliance Dealers

• Automobile/Truck Dealers

• Cellular Phones & Communications Dealers

• Computer Dealers

• Farm Equipment Dealers

• Farm Supply Dealers

• Feed & Chemical Supply Dealers

• Furniture & Bedding Dealers

• Hardware Dealers

• Heating & Air Conditioning Dealers

• Insurance Agents

• Lawn & Garden Dealers

- Office Equipment Dealers

- Paint/Wallpaper Dealers

- Petroleum/Lubricants Dealers

- Plumbing Dealers

- Real Estate Agents

- Recreational Equipment Dealers

- Seed Dealers

Why Advertise?

Advertising is a necessary and important part of a dealer's business. It helps build a vital link that leads to increased sales, new customers and improved profitability. Plus, it can provide the right image that reminds customers that you are the dealer to do business with. Further, advertising can motivate and involve your personnel to make them more informed and better promoters.

Coop Advertising

To maximize your budget, be sure you're getting your share of coop monies. You've got it coming. American businesses forfeit millions of dollars every year by forgetting to file or ignoring generous coop allowances. Most manufacturers or wholesalers, allow from 25 to 50% or more. The maximum amount is usually predicated on your purchases from the preceding year.

A good "partner" in handling your coop can be your local newspaper, radio or other media representative. They know the ins and outs of handling cooperative advertising. They'll help set-up your coop account. If necessary, many reps will even contact the manufacturer or other coop provider for you.

Benefits of Coop

It pays to utilize coop advertising. The benefits are many:

- Stretches your budget. (i.e. Your budget doubles if 50% coop is available.)

- Adds local impact to your manufacturer's national campaign.

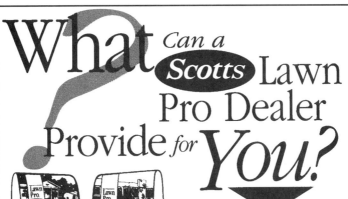

Super Turf Builder (Lawn Fertilizer)
Super Turf Builder+2°
(Weed Control + Fertilizer)

• 25% More Greening Power than Turf Builder & Turf Builder Plus 2
• Greens quickly without burning
• Develops a thicker, greener lawn

Scotts® Family Grass Seed
Sod Quality mixture that's ideal for sunny or shady areas.
• Developed for disease resistance & superior performance
• 3 lb. box

1. Exclusive, Superior Products that can only be purchased at an authorized Lawn Pro Dealer!

2. Scott's BEST products, expert advice, customer service and information on how to have a professional-looking lawn.

3. Lawn Pro fertilizers contain Scotts patented mistakeproof granules.

SpeedyGreen® Rotary Spreader
• Spreads wide - 8'
• Cushioned handle
• Holds 10,000 sq ft bag
• Scotts No-Quibble guarantee!

Prices & Products will vary -check with your local dealer for their BEST PRICE of the season!

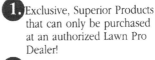

Available only at your authorized Lawn Pro dealer:

APPLE VALLEY COAST TO COAST
Times Square Ctr., NW Corner Cedar & Cty. Rd. 42 • 432-1004

AL'S LANDSCAPING
6038 Pillsbury, Minneapolis • 869-3052

CHASKA BUILDING CENTER
350 East Highway 212, Chaska • 448-6776

D&D TRUE VALUE HARDWARE
1565 Cliff Rd., Eagan • 454-2366

JERRY'S OF EDINA
5033 Vernon Ave. S., Edina • 929-4601

KRAEMER'S HARDWARE
Glen Lake Shopping Center, Minnetonka • 938-7614

KRAEMER'S HARDWARE
861 E. Lake St., Wayzata • 473-2501

LAKEVILLE COAST TO COAST
20851 Holyoke Ave., Downtown Lakeville • 469-3433

LYNDALE ACE HARDWARE
6616 S. Lyndale Ave., Richfield • 869-7555

NEW PRAGUE COAST TO COAST
1790 W. 280th St., Hwys. 19 & 13 • 758-4440

SETTERGREN'S ACE HARDWARE
5403 Penn Ave. South, Minneapolis • 922-6055

ST. LOUIS PARK TRUE VALUE
Miracle Mile Shopping Ctr, 5025 Excelsior Blvd. • 927-9701

VALLEY WEST COAST TO COAST
10530 France Ave. South, Bloomington • 884-2209

Smart dealers tie-in with group advertising to remind customers "where to buy the product."

- Reminds customers that you carry the brand; that you're the dealer to buy it from.

- Announces your seasonal and special events.

- Builds business. A consistent small space coop schedule can help establish you as the dominant dealer in your trade area for the product or service advertised.

Media Menu

Many manufacturers offer a wide variety of coop media choices. Use the one that works best for your operation:

- Newspapers and shoppers

- Radio

- TV

- Direct mail

- Outdoor advertising

Dealer Group Ads

There's savings in numbers! So if you have an opportunity to tie-in with a dealer group ad, do it. Unlike an individual dealer ad, these list all the participating dealers — usually from one region — at the bottom of the ad.

Most are large-space, special type ads that showcase the brand or product that you represent. Since the cost is shared among all dealers listed, your price is nominal.

Interestingly, some dealers decline group ads. They see the other dealers listed as "competition." Their absence, however, can cost them business. Especially knowing that one key question that prospects have is: "Where do I buy the product?" I highly recommend them. They work.

As hard as it may seem, no prospective buyer really wants your *product*. He/she wants to reduce costs, improve production, increase revenues and make a problem go away. So, make your advertising sell *solutions* to customer problems.

Ask for your coop material on computer disc, like Larson Storm Doors has available. Makes ad production easier, faster — and better.

Larson Cooperative Advertising Program.

Purpose:
To help defray some of your advertising expenses so you can increase your promotional activities beyond the restriction of your normal budget to ultimately sell more Larson products and increase your profits.

Eligibility:
All customers of Larson Manufacturing Company are eligible to participate in this cooperative advertising program provided they comply with the provisions outlined within this program.

How your account fund is determined:
Larson Manufacturing Company will pay for 50% of your advertising costs in an amount that totals up to 1% of your total dollar net purchases (based on current calender year) on all Larson products.

For Example:
If a customer buys $100,000 worth of products from Larson Manufacturing within a calender year, they can qualify for $1,000 in cooperative advertising money by spending $2,000 in advertising of Larson products. The cooperative program is only applicable if the products advertised are purchased from Larson Manufacturing Company or one of its participating distributors.

Qualifying Advertising Expenses:

1. Newspaper
2. Newspaper Supplement
3. Radio
4. Television
5. Magazines
6. Direct Mail Stuffers

Please Note: If local media is determined ineffective in your market area, you may use your cooperative advertising dollars for display samples and literature.

Also Note: Up to 50% of cooperative advertising dollars may be spent for production of broadsides, tabloids or circulars. The remaining 50% must be used for local media placement as outlined above.

Format and Layout:
1. The Larson product must receive mention, be spelled correctly and a Larson logo must also appear.

2. You must use the Larson products exact logo type. We encourage you to use our reproducible ad mats, radio and TV scripts available from us on almost all Larson products.

3. If competitive products are to be mixed in the same print ad, radio or television commercial, Larson Manufacturing will not participate.

4. If competitive products are to be mixed in the same broadsides, tabloids or circulars, they must be separated from Larson products by using a dark border at least 1/4" in width and a Larson logo must be displayed at all times.

5. The dealer cooperative advertising budget covers only standard applicable rates for space and/or broadcast times in newspaper, radio or TV ads. It does not cover preparation and production costs of ads. However, for special dealer catalogs or merchandise flyers, the budget covers only the proportionate share, paper, printing charges and freight or mail charges for distribution.

6. Larson shall be be held harmless from any claim and liability resulting from the ad unless the claim or liability is based solely upon written materials furnished by Larson Manufacturing Company.

Reimbursement And Funding Periods:
1. Proof of advertising must be made by sending the original, full-page tear sheets for all ads. All radio and television affidavits must be notarized on the script by the station. An itemized paid invoice from each medium must be submitted in addition to other support documents.

2. We encourage you to send all requests for advertising to us at the end of each month rather than turning them in at the end of the year. By doing this, you will be reimbursed sooner. All ads run in a particular year must be submitted by January 10 or they will not be accepted. Submit all requests to: Coop Claims, Larson Manufacturing Company, 2333 Eastbrook Drive, Brookings, SD 57006.

3. Cooperative Advertising credit memorandums will be issued on a quarterly basis. Materials must be received by the 10th of each month following the end of the quarter to qualify for reimbursement for that particular quarter. First quarter checks or credit memorandums are issued in April, second quarter in July, third quarter in October and fourth quarter in January.

Miscellaneous:
This cooperative advertising program is designed for use only as outlined herein.

All advertising under this program must comply with all government laws and regulations. This program is subject to revision or termination without notice.

© 1997 Larson Manufacturing Company

Larson Storm Doors. Craftsmanship in every detail.™

Sample cooperative advertising program.

Tough, Tougher, Toughest.

VALUE-CORE® 288-SS

Easy Seasonal Changes.

A VALUE-CORE™ Self-Storing storm door makes seasonal changes a breeze with tempered safety glass window and screen inserts. Strong solid wood core resists sagging, twisting and denting. Maintenance free aluminum exterior in white and earth-tone brown. Limited Lifetime PLUS Warranty.

On sale for just... **$000.00**

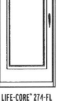

LIFE-CORE® 274-FL

Accents the Beauty of Your Home.

Show off the beauty of your primary door with a LIFE-CORE™ Full-Lite storm door. Full-length screen included. One-piece solid wood core resists sagging, twisting and denting. Maintenance-free seamless aluminum exterior. Available in white, earth-tone brown, sandstone or almond. Limited Lifetime PLUS Warranty.

On sale for just... **$000.00**

MAGNA-CORE® 236-SX

Seals Your Home Drum-tight.

Special magnetic weatherstripping seals out weather, dust, pests and quietly pulls the door closed. One-piece solid wood core, LIFETIME hinges, deadbolt lock and key. Available in white, earth-tone brown, sandstone or almond, grid and crossbuck moldings included. Limited Lifetime PLUS Warranty.

On sale for just... **$000.00**

(Dealer Name Here)

Larson Storm Doors. Craftsmanship in every detail.™

Good selling ads can help dealers boost their image — and move inventory.

Promote your people — and products — with this teamwork ad idea. Take advantage of your big plus over competition — your people. Showcase them from time to time. Besides building more awareness in your advertising, you'll instill new pride in your personnel. (What person doesn't want recognition?) First step, contact your hometown newspaper. Have them take a picture of the people you want featured.

Besides promoting products, this Teamwork ad pumps-up your people.

BECAUSE THIS YEAR MOTHER NATURE WAS JUST PRACTICING.

$00 RESERVES YOUR TORO° SNOWTHROWER FOR NEXT WINTER!

- Because of the Blizzard of '96, our entire supply of Toro snowthrowers sold-out very early this year. But there is a solution.

- Your deposit today reserves the 1997 Toro of your choice for pick-up next fall.

- Choose from a full line of Toro snowthrowers at pre-season prices with no payments or interest until April 1, 1997.*

- Hurry, this is a limited time offer. See us for details today. Because while this year's blizzard is history, next year's is on the way.

(DEALER IMPRINT HERE)

TORO

When you want it done right.

*Come in now and get pre-approved on Toro's No Payments, No Interest until April 1, 1997 financing program. This financing option is available for all units reserved now and delivered between June 1, 1996 and October 1, 1996.†

http://www.toro.com

© 1996 The Toro Company

Dealers appreciate timely marketing support, like this eye-catching Toro snowthrower ad.

11

Business-to-Business Advertising

Consistent trade advertising pays off. Here's how to make it work harder for you.

McGraw-Hill, the leader in business publishing, summed-up the need for trade advertising best. In a classic advertisement, it shows a suspicious looking buyer in a typical buyer's chair. He says to the salesman:

"I don't know who you are.
I don't know your company.
I don't know your company's product.
I don't know what your company stands for.
I don't know your company's customers.
I don't know your company's record.
I don't know your company's reputation.
Now — what was it you wanted to sell me?"

Buyers are watching budgets closer than ever. They want more information about companies and products before making a purchasing decision. They demand more reasons to purchase from you rather than your competitor. Thus the recommendation for business-to-business marketers to advertise is a sound one. Consistent advertising makes your marketing more efficient by:

• Making contact far beyond the reach of the sales force

• Arousing interest

• Generating brand awareness

• Creating leads

• Building brand preference

• Increasing sales

- Increasing market share

- Boosting profits

10 Ways to Boost Business

Once called industrial advertising and trade advertising, its new name is "business-to-business," but its purpose is the same. It means products that people buy for their companies, not for themselves. Here are ten ways you can build more satisfied customers — and profits.

1. **Draw-up a marketing plan.** Define your objectives clearly. A meaningful 12 month business plan includes: Mission statement, sales objectives, sales-promotions, budget and media plan. A written plan, no matter how short, is better than no plan.

2. **Get closer to your customer.** Start with a consistent advertising campaign. This plays an important role in the selling process. Also, have your salespeople focus on their customers' wants and needs. Help solve their problems. Buyers are looking for ways to control costs; to improve profitability. Be part of their team with relationship or partnership selling. Your customers' levels of satisfaction will be far greater when you serve them as a consulting supplier. Also, knowing many business purchases require approval from top managers, get closer to as many layers of management as possible. Go beyond the buying agent.

3. **Build customer loyalty.** Some customers are worth more than others. Reward loyalty with special treatment. High-value customers are hard to replace. Have you ever sent them a "Top 100 Dealer Award?" It's one small, effective way you can recognize top customers.

4. **Develop a prospect list.** Every company faces customer attrition. That's why you always need to be on the lookout for new business. Add any names, as you find them, to your database. Include the list of those clients you want the most.

5. **Consider a buying-incentive.** Premiums can help motivate customers. So can discounts. Rebates. Inventory clearances. Or, seasonal and special promotions. But remember. It's easy to give things away or "buy" business. The challenge is to create a compelling offer that is win-win for you *and* your customer.

6. **Power-up sales support.** In any kind of economy, selling is a challenge. That's why it's important to pump-up your salespeople every

Example of how advertising can tell a very convincing story.

way possible. One good way is to keep their sales-portfolio filled with fresh, meaningful sales support data and leave behinds. Including: Impressive looking calling cards. Product or sell sheets. Market data. Industry news. Advertising reprints — blown-up, if possible. Success stories. When they're backed with innovative selling tools, salespeople will sell more.

7. **Put a "hook" in your sales literature.** Be sales driven and ask for action in your ads and brochures. Invite the reader to phone, FAX or place an order. By including a free offer — as simple as a new product booklet or brochure — you'll build readership. Also, customers will have a closer tie with your company if they respond to your advertising.

8. **Advertise to both dealers and end-users.** When a product or brand is sold through dealers, it pays to target both dealers and end-users. Admittedly, it's a double advertising role, but studies show that sales response is far greater when both markets — dealers and end-users — are advertised to. Research also shows a side benefit. Dealers are more motivated with your product when you help drive business to them through consumer advertising. Be sure to have your sales force carry ads with them. Show buyers what your company is doing.

9. **Move fast on leads.** Don't allow leads to get cold. Whether they come from reader response cards, trade shows, salespeople or telemarketing, follow-up on them fast. Slow response is risky. By the time the requested information arrives, the recipient may have a low opinion of your company or worse, may have located a more attentive supplier.

10. **Benefit from outside help.** More and more small to midsized companies are doing what the giant corporations have always done: Outsourcing some of their marketing activities. Some of the projects include: Advertising, catalogs, brochures, newsletters, special image pieces, special events and marketing plans. Advertising specialists make valuable suppliers. They won't waste time "reinventing the wheel." For another, they'll give you an outside perspective that can't be achieved in-house. As the Wall Street Journal recently reported, the fees for a retired specialist are modest compared to the potential payoff and benefits they offer.

Here's a trade ad with a retail look. The direct mail campaign featured janitorial supplies for commercial accounts.

Writing Trade Advertising That Sells

For the most part, advertising techniques for both trade and consumer advertising are pretty much the same — like promising readers a benefit, news, testimonials, and helpful information. But make your promise specific in trade advertising, because in some cases, you're talking to engineers. Instead of generalities, point out quality, dollars saved, return-on-investment and delivery time.

To stimulate inquiries, put your free 800 number in ads and all your sales literature. When possible, include a coupon requesting more information.

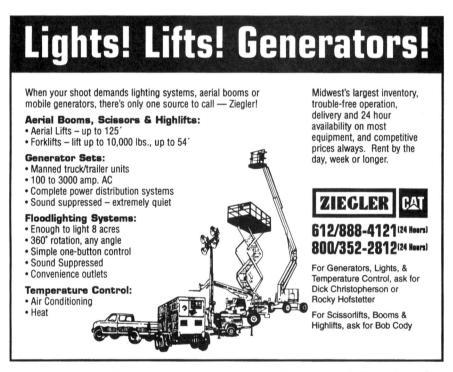

Example of an effective business-to-business directory ad. Note how the drawings help sell the equipment capabilities.

12

15 Reasons for Accelerating Your Advertising

Here's plenty of ammunition to help you "sell" top management on a major advertising commitment.

I could cry! There are still too many good companies out there, standing on the advertising sidelines. Maybe yours. For some reason or other, top management has not been *sold* on the merits of a consistent advertising program. As the person charged with the responsibility for communications in your company, there'll be times to "sell" your key people on a specific advertising project. To help you, here are 15 important reasons for investing in advertising. Check-off any of the factors that could help your company grow.

❏ **Produce immediate sales.** New sales can help generate the cash flow that your company may be looking for. With heavily advertised promotions, you'll ring the cash register for the business and profits every company needs.

❏ **Launch a new product or service.** The most effective way to roll-out a new product is with advertising fan-fare. Without it, it could take longer to get your product off the ground. (Which could be more expensive than the cost of your initial advertising.) Advertising is fundamental when it comes to new products and services.

❏ **Kick-off a major promotion.** When you've got a lot riding on a seasonal event, company milestone or special promotion, you need to make it a success. Turn-up the advertising! Too often companies hold back, and as a result, the promotion never gets off the ground.

❏ **Force distribution**. You may have some dealers that are slow in stocking your product line. One way to get their attention — and their orders — is by having customers ask for your promotion or products. Consumer advertising can heat-up the selling temperature to accomplish this.

❏ **Attract new customers**. Advertising was made for bringing in new business. And the choice is unlimited: Direct mail, radio, TV, newspapers or trade shows. Let prospects know that you'd appreciate their business.

❏ **Retain existing customers**. Building brand loyalty is an on-going job. With consistent advertising, you'll be "talking" to your customers on a regular basis. Customers get a good feeling when they see *their* brand featured.

❏ **Open doors for personal sales calls**. Advertising is a little like a friend calling ahead to introduce your company's salesperson. Your message can break the ice for a warmer first call. Perhaps its a special direct mail campaign that targets your top prospects. Or, a trade magazine ad that reaches your total market. Let advertising lead the way for your company's sales team.

❏ **Educate prospects on needs, features & benefits**. Advertising can help speed-up the buying process. When prospects know something of your company — its products, its quality, its reputation — the buying process has started. Don't assume that your prospects know all about your product line or service. Education is an on-going service.

❏ **Enhance employee pride, loyalty and morale**. A side benefit for advertising helps instill a renewed pride and enthusiasm among employees. Taking it further, if applicable, consider your people in ads.

❏ **Clear out obsolete products**. Nearly every company experiences over-stocking. That's when advertising can really show its stuff. There's a certain segment of shoppers that wait for clearance sales. Dedicate an ad or two to clearing out the back room.

❏ **Project a new corporate image**. There comes a time when every type of business from head-hunters to hardware stores should "toot" their horn. You'll want to communicate information about your organization, your products, services, people, new logo or whatever. Advertising can tell your story to your trade area — fast.

Money talks! Example of a powerful "eye-trap" to pull-in readers.

❏ **Resell lost customers**. Direct mail can help you talk directly to those customers you want back. Tell them about the new features and benefits you can offer them. There's a good chance they'll be happy to hear from you.

❏ **Offer brochures, booklets and product data**. Be sales-driven in your advertising. Always ask for action from your readers. By including a free offer on your new product booklet, for example, you'll get more readership — plus, start the buying process by putting information in your prospects' hands.

❏ **Open new markets**. In World War II, the big guns pounded the beaches before our troops landed. Let advertising be your *big guns* to soften-up your new market. It's the most effective way to let prospects know that you've landed. Knowing your budget is limited, target your media carefully. Your campaign might use direct mail, newspapers/shoppers, radio or TV.

❏ **Stand above/apart from competition**. Advertising is information. So tell your trade area about your product, service or retail operation. Advertising can help set you apart from a commodity image. Maybe you need a new brochure or booklet telling your company story. It's a corny saying, but it applies: "Don't hide your candle under a basket."

Offer brochures, booklets, etc. to keep customers informed about products and services.

13

Ring-Up More Retail

Win the "store wars" with smart merchandising and hometown customer service.

Retailing has always been a challenge. But with the dominance of Wal-Mart and the giant Do-It-Yourself hardware/lumber stores, small retailers have had to reshape, and in some cases, reinvent themselves. The survivors are competing with the giants with smart merchandising, innovative selling and stepped-up customer service and advertising.

Taking On Wal-Mart

"Wal-mart is coming! Wal-Mart is coming!" Many Main Street merchants lie down and close when they learn that Wal-Mart is targeting their trade area. And can you blame them? After all, their average store sells $15 million annually, a sum that blows most hometown retailers away. And when a new Wal-Mart goes up, it has anywhere from 50,000 to 125,000 square feet. And they have 36 departments — the equivalent of 36 stores.

This "big-time" store profile was the wake-up call for Nelson Agri-Center, a successful farm supply store in Viroqua, Wisconsin. (A dairyland community of 3,700, some 80 miles southeast of LaCrosse.)

Wal-Mart's plans to build on the west edge of town spurred Fred Nelson, then owner of the popular feed mill and supply store. Nelson's made the necessary "big-time" changes to compete more effectively. First, they eliminated a lot of items that they couldn't be price competitive on. (Including health and beauty aids and small appliances.) They extended their store hours. Importantly, they focused on customer service. (Something they were pretty good at before.)

The store, now owned by Roy Kanis, took a smaller profit on price sensitive items, like power tools and motor oil, while broadening their product range in farm tools, clothing and local crafts. The store continues its niche focus under Kanis. It has remodeled and added a complete tool rental department, which brings in many new customers. More than a True Value Hardware store and feed mill, Nelson's is a vital part of the Viroqua community. They participate in countless local events.

The results after Wal-Mart? Nelson Agri-Center's facelift and new merchandising strategies worked. They kept the giant at bay. Sales went up since Wal-Mart's arrival and importantly, profits have held up.

It's the "Super Bowl" of in-store events. Nelson's Sales Fair features a new theme each year for new-excitement.

Promotional Mix

Successful retailing requires a promotional mix. From the marketing point of view, the term *promotion* encompasses several different sets of activities:

- Advertising

- Publicity

- Personal selling

- Sales promotion

Promotion Tools for Special Store Events

To help trigger your imagination, here are some promotion tools for your special events (*Anniversary Sale, Open House,* etc.):

- Advertising specialties (Giveaways - Key chains, pens, etc.)

- Balloons

- Clown

- Contest

- Demonstrations

- Exhibits

- Food (Donuts, hot-dogs, etc.)

- Games

- Guest celebrities

- Handbills

- In-store signs

- Kiddie rides

- Name badges

- Newspaper ads

- Premiums (For prizes)

- News releases

- Remote radio broadcast

- Ribbon cutting ceremony

- Supplier (factory) representatives

- Theme idea for event

- Other _____

CREATE
FUN
AND
EXCITEMENT!

Is your store maximizing its sales opportunities? The hardware stores are experienced in suggestion or extension selling. If a customer asks for paint, the alert clerk will immediately suggest *brushes, sandpaper and paint thinner*. This is like making "two customers out of one."

Suggestion selling offers three benefits. It's a perfect win-win-win situation for the customer, salesperson and the store:

1. A service for customers who can use the tie-in items.

2. The exchange improves salesmanship for the salesperson.

3. A larger sales-ticket for the store.

How to Make "Two Customers" Out of One*

You'll be doing your customers a service by recommending tie-in items.

To go with:	Suggest:
Paint	Paint brushes, sandpaper, masking tape, paint thinner, etc.
Hammer	A screwdriver, pliers, nails
Power lawn mower	2 cycle oil, lawn bags, gloves
Fertilizer	Spreader, gloves
House plant	Plant food, potting soil, a planter
Oil change	Antifreeze flush & change, transmission oil, filters
Shoes	Hosiery, belt, slippers
Slacks	Shirt or blouse, belt
New furnace	Heat duct cleaning
Computer	Laser printer, color monitor, scanner, modem, pad
Camera	Tripod, film, zoom lens
Moving truck rentals	Pads, 2-wheel cart, packing boxes
Movie video rentals	Popcorn, candy, snacks

*Reprinted with permission from *How to Start and Run Your Own Retail Business*, by Irving Burstiner, PH.D. Copyright 1994. Published by Carol Publishing Group.

Sales and Theme Selection

Calendar Events	Seasonal/Miscellaneous Sales
Happy New Year Sale	Anniversary Sale
Valentine's Day	Truck Load Sale
Presidents' Birthdays	March Madness
St. Patrick's Day	Shower of Savings
Easter Time	Spring Fling
Mother's Day	Spring Clean-Up Sale
Memorial Day	Luau Sale
Graduation Time	Mid-Summer Sale
Flag Day	Open House
Father's Day	Manager's Sale
Independence Day	Dollar Days
County/State Fair Time	Seasonal Clean-Up
Back to School Days	Going Out for More Business Sale
Labor Day	Other_____
Columbus Day	
Election Day	
Veteran's Day	
Halloween	
Thanksgiving	
Christmas Time	

Seasonal advertising pays! Lyndale Hardware's coupon books stimulate sales in every department.

Top 10 Store Ideas

Here are today's TOP 10 STORE IDEAS — things you can do right now to accelerate more business:

1. **Build An "Everyone Sells" Store**
   ...Empower *all* employees to help, service and sell customers.

2. **Showcase Your Specials**
   ...Merchandise your best buys. Make it easy for customers to buy.

3. **Advertise Regularly**
   ...Promote your specials, seasons and image.

4. **Hold In-Store Events**
   ...People like celebrations. Move more merchandise during special events.

5. **Call Customers By Name**
   ...People like recognition. Remember customers by name.

6. **Carry Adequate Inventory**
   ...Buying right makes you more competitive. Build big displays and sell more.

7. **Suggestion Selling**
   ...Recommend related items for more sales. Customers need tie-in items.

8. **Sharpen the Saw**
   ...Keep personnel motivated by keeping them trained.

9. **Be Community Minded**
   ...Participate in local activities. The pay back is tremendous.

10. **Invite Customers to Buy**
    ...Your recommendation is valued. Help customers with buying decisions.

Bikers brake for this special sale. A good example of an organized retail ad.

PACKER SUPER BOWL TAILGATE PARTY

**Tackle the Nelson Agri-Center
Packer Super Bowl Tailgate Party
Friday, January 24th
11 a.m. until food is gone!**

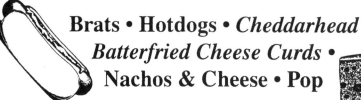

Brats • Hotdogs • *Cheddarhead*
Batterfried Cheese Curds •
Nachos & Cheese • Pop

**Shop Corner Gifts and receive a FREE Packer
Carnation with a $10 purchase or more!**
(While Supplies Last!)

Nelson Agri-Center
217 N. Center   Viroqua, WI   637-2192

Smart retailers tie-in with local and national events. This "Tailgate Party" helped produce plus-business for Nelson Agri-Center.

14

The Power of Sales Promotion

Separate yourself from competition with effective promotional tools and special events.

Every business can benefit from sales promotion. Its activities can range from a simple, inexpensive promotional product — like a ballpoint pen — to an attention getting special event with all the bells and whistles.

Sales promotion is:

...a relatively short-term activity.

...used in order to stimulate some specific action.

...directed towards the sales force, distribution channels or consumers.

The Power of Promotion

Here's what sales promotion can do for your company. It can:

• Introduce new products or services

• Drive sales of existing products

• Attract new customers

• Expand markets

• Support and motivate sales personnel

• Build overall sales volume

• Showcase your company at special events

There's been a shift in budgets. Marketers are spending more on promotion; less in measured media advertising. The erosion of mass media effectiveness has benefited sales promotion, including the use of premiums that entice consumers with value-added offers.

Multifaceted

Sales promotion is multifaceted. Here are the many different ways it can impact your business:

- *Programs and Promotions* — The customers of today are different than the customers of yesterday. They expect more! That's why the marketplace is in such a promotional frenzy. In both retailing and trade, the price-sensitive customer wants *everything* on sale. That's why many industries have stepped up their promotion and program efforts. (Especially fast-food stores and the communications companies.)

  Make sure your next promotion is a winner. Here are some ways to build more awareness — and sales:

  1. Give your promotion a "name," or "theme." (A "handle" the customer can grab on to.)

  2. Make it exciting! Give your promotion the "look" of excitement in your advertising or mailing piece.

  3. Include an ending date to spur action.

  4. Feature at least one "hot" special to get attention.

  5. Consider a premium tie-in for added value.

  6. Give yourself an adequate budget to make the promotion appealing. (And the right media mix to deliver your message to the right prospects.)

- *Promotional Products* — Often called "ad specialties," merchandise incentives can influence behavior among consumers, dealers and employees by offering a specific reward for a specific activity.

- *Sales Support* — Selling has always been a challenge. So, the more "tools" you supply your sales people, the better for your company. Sales support includes:

  1. Sales meetings. (To stimulate, educate and motivate.)

  2. Sales aids. (Calling cards, product literature, catalog sheets, presentation material, industry trends, ad reprints, etc.)

A winning promotion! Emma Krumbee's Scarecrow Festival was named one of the "Top 25 Group Tour Festivals and Events."

- *Collateral Material.* Every business needs support material to help influence the buying process. It includes: P.O.P. for retailers, brochures, product literature and print materials of every kind to support your promotional efforts.

- *Packaging Design* — Make it eye-catching to build awareness for your business. Packaging includes labels, boxes, containers, retail packs, plastic and poly bags and carton inserts. For best results, use an outside source for this important area of marketing.

- *Direct Mail* — At the expense of mass media, direct mail has become an important marketing niche. Whether targeted to consumers or trade, your promotion or message can generate the response you want. Unlike radio or TV, you "talk" to just the people you want to reach.

- *Performance Programs* — Sales stalled? Quality slipping? Work accidents climbing? Improve performance with employee incentives and awards. It's human nature. People turn-up their performance when challenged — and rewarded. Occasionally you need to motivate the sales force, for example, to reach higher selling levels. The incentives can range from certificates or trophies, to trips, premiums or cash. (Remarks: Incremental business can often pay for an incentive program, making it self-liquidating.)

- *Special Events* — Meetings, trade shows, in-store events and special event marketing all require plenty of lead-time. Make them special; make them memorable. Make them pay off!

The author, right, and colleagues celebrate Ag Day with milk. (A special marketing event Hill helped develop.)

Planning Your Promotion

To assure successful promotions, follow these four planning steps:

1. *Objective* - What's the purpose? To create new customers? Or, deliver a 15% increase in sales over last year? Be specific in describing your goals.

2. *Business Plan* - How will you build and execute the promotion? What's your drawing card? Incentives? (Discounts, specials, etc.) What's your theme? Take time to prepare a "road map."

3. *Media Plan* - How will you reach your customers? What's your media mix? (Direct mail, newspaper, radio, etc.)

4. *Budget* - How much can you spend? It goes without saying that "you can't spend $10 to bring in $5 worth of business." Be business-like and realistic in developing your budget.

Incentives

Incentives are used to motivate customers to buy and sales people and other employees to work more effectively. Incentives take the form of merchandise, travel, cash, "perks," — even sporting event tickets. Depending on your objective — and your budget — here are some of the different kinds of incentives to help drive more business:

- Discounts
- Cents-off coupons
- Rebates
- Free offer
- Premium tie-in
- Sweepstakes
- Inventory clearance
- Trial offer

Promotional Products Marketing

Was there ever a day when you haven't come across a calendar, coffee mug, ballpoint pen, a cap or a T-shirt bearing an advertiser's name or logo? When these items are given to you free, they're called *ad specialties*. However, if you're asked to make a purchase or do something to earn them, they become *premiums*. Ad specialties, premiums, business gifts, awards and commemoratives — they are all examples of promotional products. Their exposure is universal.

15,000 Choices

Which ones to use? There are an estimated 15,000 different types of promotional products. The top five product categories in terms of sales are:

1. *Wearables* - Including T-shirts, baseball caps, jackets, sweatshirts, fanny packs and sun glasses.

2. *Writing Instruments* - Ballpoint pens are a favorite traffic builder. Or, use trendy brand name pens to impress top customers.

3. *Recognition Awards & Trophies* - Great motivators for employees or customers. From wall plaques to clocks.

4. *Glassware/Ceramics* - Glass sets, crystal pieces and colorful beverage mugs.

5. *Calendars* - A traditional ad specialty item, many companies promote with calendars every year.

25 Promotional Product Ideas

Here's just a "starter list" from the wide variety of promotional products that are offered to businesses and non-profit organizations. Prices can range from under a dollar to well over $10 per recipient. Your local advertising specialties representative can supply you with full color catalogs for additional ideas.

- Baseball Caps

- T-Shirts

- Coaches Jackets

- Fannypacks

- Calendars

- Computer Accessories (Disk guards, mouse pads)

- Phone Cards (Free calling time)

- Voice Activated Items (Business cards, birthday cards)

- Pocket Calculators

- Gym Bags

- Sun Glasses, Umbrellas
- Beverage Mugs (for home, office & vehicle)
- Writing Instruments (From inexpensive ballpoint pens to desk sets)
- Key Tags & Luggage Tags
- Flashlights
- Rulers, Yardsticks
- Beverage and Picnic Coolers
- Barbecue Tools & Aprons
- Food Gifts
- Desk/Office/Business Accessories
- Games, Toys, Playing Cards
- Recognition Awards & Trophies
- Jewelry, Clocks & Watches
- Buttons, Badges, Ribbons
- Refrigerator Magnets

Beverage mugs make good incentives. They lend an added value to your product.

Yardstick Becomes "Snowgauge"

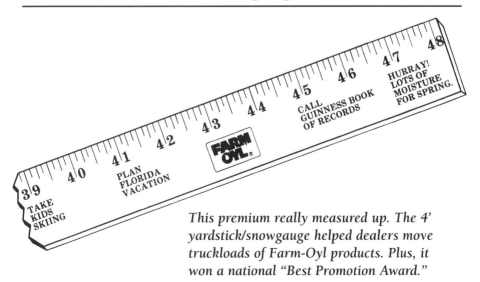

This premium really measured up. The 4' yardstick/snowgauge helped dealers move truckloads of Farm-Oyl products. Plus, it won a national "Best Promotion Award."

Thistle feeders on thale.

20% OFF THISTLE FEEDERS DURING OUR 5TH ANNIVERSARY SALE.

Five years of doing business with fellow bird enthusiasts. That calls for a celebration. So, from April 11-14, we're bringing prices down for the long-awaited spring. In addition to sale priced thistle feeders, you'll find lower prices on bluebird houses and kits, oriole feeders, birding books, and plenty of other birding tools. We've also planned a special attraction. On April 14th, from 1-3 p.m., the Raptor Center will be displaying birds of prey at both our Bloomington and White Bear Lake stores. Don't mith it.

WILD BIRD S·T·O·R·E

Mall of America · 854-5485   35W & 98th St · 884-4103
White Bear Lake · Hwy 120 & Cty Rd E · 770-7516

A 5th Anniversary is an important milestone and a good reason to promote your retail operation.

15

Need A Corporate Facelift?

Whether a new logo or a total company revitalization, change takes commitment — and a new perspective.

To grow in today's competitive marketplace, businesses of every size are being forced to reshape themselves. No matter what you call it — streamlining, reengineering or revitalization — change is never easy. Even implementing a new logo can build new awareness for your company. A new "look" offers your company a "fresh start." And when done right, it instills a renewed pride and enthusiasm among employees.

Look for Warning Signs

How do you know if you need a new corporate identity? Or a company change-over? Short of holding a formal performance review of your business — that could be timely and expensive — here's my laundry list of warning signs that may indicate a change is in order. Merely place a check mark beside each item — concerns or problems — that may need addressing. (✔)

❑ Static sales

❑ Shrinking profits

❑ Uncommitted employees

❑ "Walls" between departments

❑ Ineffective distribution system

❑ Few new products

❑ Growing customer complaints

- ❏ Losing loyal customers

- ❏ Few new customers

- ❏ Uncaring or unresponsive image

- ❏ Heightened competition

- ❏ Old technology

- ❏ No marketing plan

- ❏ No company mission

- ❏ High price image

- ❏ Poor advertising response

- ❏ Lackluster communications

- ❏ Outdated logo. (Or no logo)

- ❏ Low morale; little teamwork

If your company can relate to five or more of the above concerns/problems, you may want to consider a revitalization project. There's a good chance it will involve communications and employee motivation. From my past experience, I've found there are four areas that companies can easily identify with. In nautical terms, they're listed from major to minor projects.

1. **Leaky ship**. Experiencing sales leakage or sinking profits? You're not alone. Many famous companies have had this same problem. After an overhaul, they rebounded. So can you.

2. **Faulty compass**. Drifting businesses need new hands-on direction. Like a practical marketing plan to lead you out of rough waters. Before a whirlpool is sighted.

3. **Underpowered**. Turn-on the after-burner to pull ahead of the pack. Rev-up your systems and strategies with new technologies to make your organization more productive and competitive.

4. **Rusty scupper**. Some minor maintenance — like image polishing and people motivation — may improve the looks of your business. Maybe your sales team needs motivating. Or perhaps a fresh advertising look is needed to create more awareness and sales.

Outside Perspective

Sometimes companies are able to draw on their own people to correct the required changes. But in most cases, it takes an outsider to effectively implement a corporate facelift.

Sources include, from most to least expensive:

- Business consultant

- Advertising agency

- Research firm

- Advertising specialist

When to introduce your new look, logo or revitalization program? The best time to kick-off your new corporate facelift is when you have something special to offer. (i.e. Anniversary, sales event, new product or new service intro, etc.) To run just a plain "look at us," campaign is too self-serving. Tie it in with a promotion when your customers will benefit even more.

6 Turn-Around Tips

A corporate facelift could be your answer for motivated personnel and more satisfied customers. But first, get everyone involved. Make the entire operation part of the "new commitment to change." Here are six tips for improving your company performance.

1. **Create a caring image**. How do customers perceive your company? A simple in-house survey can give you some insight. Or better, an unbiased research project will show your strengths and weaknesses. The goal is to correct any negative feelings toward your company. (i.e. Pricing may be a factor. Or personnel or hard nose policies.)

2. **Introduce enterprise thinking.** Are there any "walls" between departments? Knock 'em down! Employee bickering may be holding you back. Customers can sense inside tension. Today's business climate demands new approaches and new ways of getting things done. It requires *"enterprise thinking,"* an attitude that focuses on the *entire business* — integrating sales, marketing, advertising and operations. This team concept promises profitability through shared information, elimination of duplicate efforts, increased communications and heightened efficiency.

3. **Be customer driven.** Most organizations call their order department, "Customer Service." Broaden it. Make it company wide. Empower *every* employee to help service customers. Today, the public expects more. Make your company *customer driven*. Strengthen the way you greet, meet and service customers.

4. **Use relationship selling.** Get closer to your customers. The days of "order taking" are over. Sales objections can be easier overcome through *relationship selling*. Find your customer's "pain" or "problems." Then, help solve those problems. Even when a prospect doesn't buy or sign an order today, thank them for their consideration. They'll know you're interested in their business. Hopefully, they'll be back later as a happy customer.

5. **Develop effective communications.** Good communications are vital to business success. By using today's technologies and by out-sourcing special projects, one person in a small to midsized company — you — can effectively organize and manage your marketing communications activities. Including advertising, sales promotion, public relations — all facets of communications. (See Chapter One for more detailed ways to organize and operate your advertising function.)

6. **Hold frequent updates or meetings.** Make your company more unified with meaningful feedback. And be sure to hold a "celebration meeting" before your corporate facelift is introduced. A new "look" offers your company a "fresh start." So take advantage of it by holding an in-house rally. (Mary Kay and other sales oriented companies do it all the time.)

You're Not Alone

Doing business in today's hyper-competitive marketplace isn't easy. This is true for all size companies — small, midsized, even the giants. General Motors, for example, has under-gone a mammoth reengineering project. (People *and* products.) Research showed that GM was perceived as uncaring, out-of-touch and unresponsive in the late 1970's and into the 80's. This has been referred to as General Motor's "embarrassing phase."

Since then, however, they have corrected many of the problems. Importantly, they have turned the negative perception around. To further strengthen brand loyalty, GM has launched a major corporate campaign to re-build the GM image — and the GM market share. GM's Saturn venture is the envy of the industry. Its marketing message rings true for

America's new small auto maker:

"SATURN...
A Different Kind of Company. A Different Kind of Car."

Other organizations with revitalization programs include:

• Apple Computer, Inc.

• AT&T

• IBM

• P&G

• U.S. Postal Service

• Pillsbury

• Burroughs Corp.

• True Value Hardware (Cotter Co.)

When it comes to change, you're not alone. Everybody's doing it.

The Value of Logos

The purpose of a logo or corporate identity is to make it easy for customers to do business with you. The right logo drives sales. The wrong one can hold you back or make you look outdated.

A potential customer's first impression of a company is through its logo — whether on a direct mail piece, calling card or on a sign at your place of business.

Regardless of your business size — from home based to major operations — you want a modern looking logo that shows you're in business to stay. Here are some tips in developing a new logo.

1. **Go outside.** Too many businesses try to do it themselves — and they fall short. You want an *outside perspective* to give you the best results. Sources to use from least to most expensive:

   • Advertising specialist

   • A qualified artist

   • Advertising agency

   • Corporate design firm

2. **Lend direction.** Before any design can be put to paper, logo direction needs to be established. Cost? How extensive will it be used? Also, the designer needs background information on your company. (i.e. Position in market. Company's focus. Goods and services. Current image among customers. Competitive advantages, etc.)

3. **Simple is smart.** Over-designing a logo is common. But the last thing you need is a "complicated" image piece. Importantly, you want a modern, progressive looking logo that best represents your company — and will take you into the 21st Century. You want a logo that "fits" your company.

4. **Logo conversion plan.** To maximize your efforts, set up a time table for converting your new logo. For example, when do you want it to appear on packaging? In ads? Buildings? Trucks? Also, letterheads, forms, etc. Remember that a logo change takes time.

5. **Commitment to renewal.** A new logo offers your company an opportunity for a "fresh" start. It can instill a renewed pride and sales enthusiasm among employees. Also, provide an extra awareness to your company through advertising, merchandising and promotion. Make it drive sales for you by giving it as much exposure as possible. (i.e. Send out a news release to the media; promote it in your newsletter or, even in a letter.)

Waving A New Logo

Sharing a new logo with customers is a good way to maximize your company's new look. That's what **Wave Car Wash**, Edina, Minnesota, did. To introduce their new logo, they mailed to all their Club "W" members their new identity with a short explanation about the change, as below:

"**A company logo is like a dependable car...**
A new one is nice after nine years of service!"

(Proudly under the same management!)

The **WAVE** Car Wash

Proud of our tradition.
Excited about our future.

Logo Review (Simple Is Smart)

Southdale Pet Hospital

Before. . .   *. . . and after. Note how the modern, updated logo suggests speed.*

Changing with the times: 3M logos, from left , in 1910, 1950, 1961 and — far right — current logo.

An ideal time to develop or update your mission statement is during a corporate facelift. It can help re-define your organization's way of doing business.

Mission Statement: *"A formal statement of objectives and purposes of an organization, orienting team members about its business philosophy, policies and target."*

Mission Statements can be concise, like these examples:

"Focus on delivering value to customers."

Local Hardware Store

"To provide the freshest, tastiest bagels at a competitive price."

Local Bagel Bakery

"To meet our customers' needs by providing quality products, programs and services."

Heating & Air Conditioning Company

Some organizations prefer to spell their mission statement out, such as this example by Midway Container, St. Paul, Minnesota.

Mission Statement

Midway Container, Inc. is an organization of employees and shareholders who have combined their resources to pursue a common goal.

What We Do - Our common goal is to provide solutions for our customers' packaging needs through new product development and emphasizing consistent, high quality services.

Why We Do It - We pursue this goal to earn a profit, which allows us to reward our shareholders and employees and to make a contribution to our society.

How We Do It - Four principles guide our actions:

- **Customer Satisfaction** - Providing the best possible quality, service and value to the greatest number of people. Doing whatever is reasonable, and sometimes unreasonable, to make certain each customer's needs are met each and every day.

- **Integrity** - doing what is right. Caring about the dignity and rights of each individual. Acting fairly and responsibly with all parties. Being a good citizen in the communities in which we operate.

- **Teamwork** - Understanding that we must work together if we are to be successful. Realizing that each individual must contribute to the team to remain a member of the team.

- **Excellence** - Striving to perform every job or action in a superior way. Being innovative, seeking new and better ways to get things done. Helping all individuals to become the best that they can be in their jobs and careers.

Once We've Done It - When we achieve our goal, good things happen; sales increase, profits are made, shareholders and employees are rewarded, jobs are created, our communities benefit, we have fun and our customers have met their needs.

Corporate Image Piece

Every company, regardless of size, has need for a timely corporate image piece. A small company, to become better known; a big company to maintain its image.

Besides showcasing your plusses to customers it can be an excellent promotion tool for your sales staff. Types of image pieces can include:

- Company brochure

- Newsletter

- Special milestone event

- New product or service introduction

- Small, pocket size memo book

- Sales event literature

- Annual report

Many businesses have learned that to qualify for bids, a brochure with their capabilities — plant or warehouse size, volume output, etc. — can be an advantage. (This is the kind of literature that most buyers look for.)

We offer business mailers a partnership of practical information, exceptional service and sensible prices.

BRAEMAR *MAILING*

Braemar Mailing Service, Inc.
7065 Washington Ave S
Edina MN 55439-2417
612/828-9755 Fax 612/828-6891

Don't be afraid to make your image piece a selling-piece, like this brochure for Braemar Mailing.

16

A Guide to Publicity and Newsletters

"Toot" your corporate horn to gain more awareness. Great way to boost employee morale, also.

Good news! Every organization has a story to tell. That's why you'll want to communicate information about your...

...People

...New product

...Special event

...New milestone

...Industry breakthrough

Two of the most effective ways to communicate your good news is with "free" publicity and newsletters. Let's take them one by one.

Publicity

The media welcomes newsworthy announcements and feature stories. But it's up to you, as the person responsible for communications in your company, to initiate the "good news." To produce the best results, cover all the media bases, including: Newspapers, shoppers, business and trade magazines and radio and TV. Also, be sure to alert your trade association(s) — and customers. The more exposure, the better.

Granted, it takes some effort to prepare a news release or a feature story about a new happening at your company. But publicity can pay big dividends. For one thing, there's a good chance your PR story will reach more than your regular customers. You'll also be talking to *new* prospects and maybe some former customers. And here's the kicker. Your "free" advertising — publicity — may gain more readership than your paid ads. (Editorial copy is a news format vs. advertising that is totally biased.)

News Release Format

Contact: Name
Company
Address
Phone & Fax Number

For Immediate Release
(Date)

SUMMARY HEADLINE
Date Line — News Release follows beginning with who, what, when, where and how. Then, important information followed by supplementary information and concluding with a brief summary of what your company does, etc. (End).

Constructing A News Release

1. Source of information

2. Release date

3. Headline (That sums up story.)

4. Date line

5. Body copy of news release

Key Points

1. Double space and leave wide margins

2. Make paragraphs short and to the point

3. Conclude with word "End"

4. Have release proof-read

5. Mail or fax to a specific person

6. Telephone follow-up to see if person received material

7. Include a color or B&W photo if applicable (4x5)

American Institute of Small Business

7515 Wayzata Blvd.
Suite 201
(612) 545-7001

Minneapolis, Minnesota 55426
WATS 800-328-2906
FAX 612-545-7020

NEWS RELEASE

FOR IMMEDIATE RELEASE

FOR MORE INFORMATION:

Max Fallek (612) 545-7001

MAKING APPLICATIONS TO BANKS, LENDING INSTITUTIONS OR FOR SBA LOANS ARE MADE EASIER WITH BUSINESS PLAN EXAMPLE. . . .

Mpls., Mn. . . . . .Companies and individuals seeking a loan for either business expansion or a new business start-up will find it much easier to obtain such a loan simply by using a Business Plan example developed by the American Institute of Small Business. The Institute's plan is in the format required by banks, lending institutions and the SBA.

Used successfully in a special test program, the AISB Business Plan example comes complete with an Executive Summary, Mission Statement, Marketing Plan, Advertising & PR Plans, Production Plan, Funding Sources, Competitive Strengths and Weaknesses, Key Employees, Advisors and much more. It also includes Profit and Loss, Balance Sheet and Cash Flow spreadsheets for three years.

The Business Plan sells for $29.95 and is available from the American Institute of Small Business, 7515 Wayzata Blvd., Mpls. Mn. 55426 or call toll free at 800-328-2906.

NOTE TO EDITORS: BUSINESS PLAN SAMPLE AVAILABLE TO EDITORS

Sample news release by American Institute of Small Business

Newsletters

A valuable communications tool that many organizations use is a newsletter. Besides building company awareness, it can provide the news and information that customers — and employees — may need. Trade associations effectively use them to involve and motivate members about upcoming meetings, member profiles, industry news, goals and progress. Also, to recruit new members. They can be as simple as a two sided 8-1/2x11 format, to a larger 4-8 page newsletter. (If too many pages, they become more of a "magazine," which is a different format.) Some tips about producing newsletters:

- Use an 8-1/2x11 format.

- Black type on ivory paper is the most economical way to go.

- Produce it monthly or quarterly. Be consistent.

- Make it newsy. (4-5 minutes is the average time readers spend with newsletters.)

- Use pictures and captions.

Make your newsletter "chatty" and timely, like this one for the American Seminar Leaders Association.

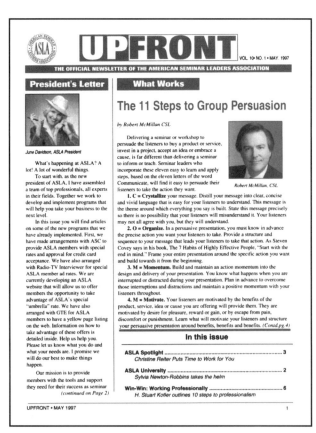

An image builder for nearly 30 years, Byerly's newsletter/magazine focuses on food, fun and life.

Headlines make ads work. Like this one for Bruegger's Bagels that ran in "Savory 4/color."

17

Smart Marketing Ideas

Beanie Babies. Hamburger Helper. Milk Mustaches. What's the connection? Some innovative ideas that worked. Now let's start working on yours.

No one has a monopoly on good ideas. But to make them pay, they need to be developed and approved. The approval part, which involves top management, can be the toughest hurdle. Many a great promotion or advertising campaign is collecting dust on a top shelf, somewhere, because the key decision maker didn't recognize its potential. Or, it wasn't properly "sold." So as the communications person in your organization, get ready for a challenge when you put your ideas across. To sell your idea or project:

1. **Be prepared.** Know the benefits and disadvantages, if any. Have all the facts on your idea or campaign.

2. **Be determined.** Be ready to hear "No." A good salesman makes his or her best pitch after the prospect says: "No."

3. **Make your presentation count.** Be in charge when you're "on stage."

Don't take it personal if your project is turned down. Many of them will be. It is top management's job to sift through the myriad of proposals and go with what they feel is best for the organization.

Here are some ideas that got approved and made it big in the marketplace.

Milk - What a Surprise!

Have you had one lately? Milk mustaches are trendy. The "Milk, What A Surprise!" campaign, which features celebrities sporting milk mustaches to encourage milk consumption, has been successful. Consumers are noticing the ads and taking a new look at milk. (One goal was to change attitudes about milk.) Celebrities, ranging from San Francisco 49'ers quarterback Steve Young to model/mother Christie Brinkley, have appeared in the campaign wearing the classic "badge" of milk enjoyment and sharing their personal milk testimonies.

Oreck Cleans Up

Oreck's free trial offer to put an eight pound vacuum cleaner in homes for 15 days got the attention every advertiser would like. No fancy jingle, like Hoover uses, David Oreck, president, is the spokesman. He delivers on radio a hard-hitting, news type commercial that is selling product. One of the keys is the consistency of the campaign. Unlike many advertisers who keep changing their theme or selling ideas, Oreck has been steadfast in their commercials. Like Hoover, Oreck is becoming a household name.

DieHard Lives On

Can a name make a product? Yes! The DieHard brand strengthened Sears automotive department. And the Sears merchandisers were smart enough to position it as their top-of-the-line battery. (As opposed to making it a price fighter.) Like an arrow to a target, the brand quickly hit the bullseye with consumers. The name — DieHard — says it all. It leads the industry in battery sales. Diehard separated itself from other brands in this highly competitive commodity product line. Today, the DieHard brand is synonymous with Sears. A smart marketing idea.

Hamburger's Helping Hand

Even the giant marketers can miss the mark. But luckily, General Mills changed directions to create one of the most popular products in the food industry — **Hamburger Helper**. Originally called "Betty Crocker Noodles Romanoff," the product was targeted to an affluent consumer. The advertising showed the meal being served with wine and candles. There was no emphasis on convenience. Sales were disappointing. Then, follow-up research suggested a new direction. Research showed that busy families didn't want snob appeal tuna noodle dishes. They wanted quick, inexpensive ways to serve ground beef. After all, families pre-

With all the milk I drink, my name might as well be Calcium Ripken, Jr. Really, I'm a huge milk fan. Besides being loaded with calcium, there's nothing like it when it's ice cold. Which is why I drink the recommended 3 glasses a day. And as you'd probably guess, I'm not one to miss a day.

MILK
Where's *your* mustache?™

A break-through concept puts more milk on the table — and on famous faces.

pared an average of three meals a week with hamburger. General Mills repositioned the product. They came up with a new name and packaging design. They called it what it is — **Hamburger Helper**. The rest is history.

The Beanie Baby Craze

They're among the most loyal fans anywhere. They stand in lines for hours to collect them. They're the young kids, teenagers, mothers and grandmothers who are looking for the special Beanie Baby — from Speedy Turtle to Inky Octopus — that will start, augment or complete their collection. And what a collection! There are over a hundred of the colorful animals that Ty Inc., Oakbrook, Illinois, created. Each has a nickname, birthdate and a corresponding poem. For example, Blackie the Bear was born 7/15/94. And who knows. His value may escalate if he's retired like Slither Snake is.

LITTLE CREATURES; BIG DEMAND!

And the timing couldn't have been better for McDonald's. They launched a Mini-Beanie-Babies craze. To get one of the mini-versions customers needed to purchase a Happy Meal. Smaller than the original collection, McDonald's promotion showcased ten separate collectibles. One Minneapolis area store reported moving out a five week supply of the little incentives, in three days. This proved to be another smart marketing idea for Ty, Inc. and for McDonald's who had the foresight to tie in with one of the hottest promotion ideas in years.

Duets and Duets II

Frank Sinatra showed the marketing world how to revive a mature brand. (Which happened to be Mr. Sinatra, himself.) By collaborating with other singers, his Duet series attracted new fans and pleased his old ones. The spotlight was off Sinatra as a solo singer and on a fresh new twosome, such as Frank Sinatra/Lorrie Morgan. Great strategy.

Interestingly, due to conflicting schedules, the two singers didn't always "sing" together. Many of the voice tracks were recorded in separate cities, then blended to together on the master track. The duet idea was an ideal way to strengthen Sinatra's performance, as he was in his 70's when he recorded the series.

18

How One Company Drums-Up Business

Learn how to compete with the giants — like this St. Paul innovator does — in America's top tractor market.

It's a classic case study. The kind that the Harvard Business School loves to illustrate. It started in St. Paul in 1929. Like Henry Ford, The Farm-Oyl Company's founder had a big dream. But instead of building automobiles, Charlie Ekstrom, a young entrepreneur, dreamed of building the hardest working tractor oil in the marketplace. He named both his company and his brand, "Farm-Oyl," which today has a federally registered trademark. And he refused to follow the industry's path of selling *commodity* items. By producing *value-added* products, his brand became a major player in the lubricants industry. Charlie Ekstrom's dream came true. He "built" the hardest working oil and grease in the marketplace.

About Farm-Oyl

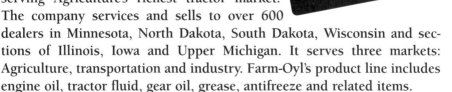

Headquartered in St. Paul, Minnesota, Farm-Oyl is a lubricants manufacturer and marketer serving Agriculture's richest tractor market. The company services and sells to over 600 dealers in Minnesota, North Dakota, South Dakota, Wisconsin and sections of Illinois, Iowa and Upper Michigan. It serves three markets: Agriculture, transportation and industry. Farm-Oyl's product line includes engine oil, tractor fluid, gear oil, grease, antifreeze and related items.

As Agribusiness knows, the farm market has always been a challenge. The Farm-Oyl brand has prevailed, however, despite the 1930's depression, recessions, government crop and dairy cut-backs, droughts and most recently, the worst flooding in history. Nothing defeats them.

The Farm-Oyl brand is sold by farm equipment dealers, service repair shops, hardware and farm supply stores, oil jobbers, feed, seed and ag-chemical dealers. Interestingly, the brand is found in many of the stores that it competes with. What's this? The John Deere, Case IH, New Holland and Agco tractor stores are owned by independent businessmen. Besides stocking their own O.E.M. brand — i.e., Deere engine oil — many of the dealers also feature the Farm-Oyl brand which has a universal appeal. Additionally, the Farm-Oyl brand competes with the oil conglomerates, including Mobil, Shell, Amoco and Texaco.

Over the years the Farm-Oyl brand grew through:

- High performance products

- Innovative promotions

- Lubricants seminars

- Merchandising support

- A close relationship with dealers

- Loyal customers

High Visibility Advertising

From its very beginning in 1929, the Farm-Oyl brand captured its market's attention. It all started with yellow and black barn signs. They were the company's first advertising campaign. And it worked. The eye-catching signs that saturated the Minnesota country

side helped call attention to the new brand and sales soon followed. Since that first experience with some basic advertising, the Farm-Oyl Company's marketing strategy has always been: *High visibility at low cost.*

Innovative Marketing

The company is both a business-to-business and end-user advertiser. It uses the *"push/pull"* marketing concept that P&G is famous for. First, *"push"* the product through the distribution pipeline. Then, with aggressive consumer advertising and promotions, help retailers *"pull"* the product out of their stores. Unlike Farm-Oyl, many companies are unwilling

EXPAND YOUR MARKET WITH OYL-POWER!

EVEN CANTERBURY DOWNS RUNS ON FARM-OYL!

More than Agriculture Runs on Farm-Oyl.

Is your store looking for ways to boost business? One proven way is to expand Farm-Oyl sales activity **outside** the store — outside Agriculture.

Who are the best prospects in your trade area? Look around. Farm-Oyl goes wherever quality lube oils are needed:

- AUTOMOBILES
- TRUCKS & BUSSES
- MANUFACTURING
- CONSTRUCTION
- LOGGING
- LAWN & GARDEN
- SCHOOLS, INSTITUTIONAL & MISC. BUSINESSES
- YOUR LOCAL TOWNSHIP OR COUNTY

The lube oil market is huge. And you can cut your share of the pie as big as you want with Farm-Oyl products. Many dealers are successfully marketing over 20,000 annual gallons.

No one offers a more complete line of lube oils for **any** industry — than The Farm-Oyl Company.

There's never been a better time for Farm-Oyl.

The FARM-OYL Company
2333 Hampden Avenue
Saint Paul, MN 55114

The "break-away" campaign. Farm-Oyl challenges dealers to expand to money-making off-farm opportunities.

to complete the "push/pull" equation. They fall short in their efforts to help dealer's *pull* product out of stores.

Farm-Oyl is a proven marketing innovator in many areas, including:

- Product technology

- Packaging

- Sales promotion

- Advertising

- In-store merchandising

Staying Power

The Farm-Oyl Company is a good example how an independent brand, smartly marketed, can build market share and loyal customers in almost any industry. Today, many third generation families are among the company's biggest brand users.

How does the farm industry rate Farm-Oyl's performance in the marketplace? Pretty high, when you ask Mel Ptacek, spokesman for the nation's largest retail group of tractor dealers, the Minnesota/South Dakota Farm Equipment Association. Farm-Oyl, noted Ptacek, has staying power. "They're a viable supplier and long time dealer supporter. When the market gets tougher, the need for Farm-Oyl's oil and grease products gets stronger," Ptacek said. "With the machinery glory days over, lubrication maintenance is more important than ever. Farm-Oyl's product line — lube oil, grease, antifreeze and related products — is the basic bread and butter line, along with other parts, that is making good money for our dealers."

The Farm-Oyl Mystique

One side benefit the company enjoys is a mystique that its name, "Farm-Oyl," has conjured up. Most people assume it is a national brand. Industry experts have noted that it perfectly describes its use to the farm community — farm oil. And its spelling of the word *"Oyl,"* has influenced many rural youngsters. Teachers have had to point out that "oil" is the dictionary spelling, and *"Oyl,"* with a "y," is the Farm-Oyl brand spelling that appears on packaging and in advertising.

HOW TO GET A BIGGER SHARE OF TODAY'S $6.5 BILLION PARTS AFTERMARKET

Build more satisfied customers and profits with Premiere Engine Oil and AG Master Tractor Fluid — unmatched in specifications and performance.

Farm-Oyl's World Class Lubricants Can Carry You to New Highs in Marketing Success and Brand Loyalty

HOW TO BECOME A WORLD CLASS LUBRICANTS MARKETER

...and Double Your Volume

Contrary to popular beliefs, oil does not have to be sold on "price." The Farm-Oyl Company has helped increase its dealers' market share with higher, not lower, value-added lubricants. We can help you go after the huge aftermarket business. Even double your present volume. Write for our FREE booklet on how to become a world class lubricants marketer.

The Farm-Oyl Company • 2333 Hampden Avenue • St. Paul, MN 55114

Effective advertising connects, touches a nerve and motivates, like this trade ad does (Note the FREE booklet offer.)

Sales brochures require good design to draw-in readers. This example shows all the signs of a good one.

19

Draw On Experience of People You Respect

Hit a creative wall? Stumped on a project? No Problem! Form a Mastermind Group for ideas, answers and motivation.

Medicine. Football. Advertising. What's the connection? Winners rarely go it alone. Smart, talented people from all fields draw on experience for help. What doctor, for example, hasn't called in a specialist for a second opinion? And have you noticed how many NFL teams are using the famous West Coast offense? And the most successful advertising people have always reached out for help when they hit the proverbial "creative wall." So you'll want to create your own "Mastermind Group" — people you respect. People that motivate you.

Your Mastermind Group

There'll come a time when you need some advice or feedback, on a project you're working on. With a Mastermind Group in place, you'll have no problem in getting the information you need. The person you turn to could be in your place of business. Or just a phone or FAX away. The sources include:

- Co-workers
- Outside friends
- Suppliers
- Trade associations

- Seminars and workshops
- Breakfast meetings
- Advertising specialists

If you're already networking, keep it up. By drawing on the experience of people you respect, you'll improve your skills and performance. (And help your company be more productive.)

One valuable tip. After you have done your rough thinking and are ready to put it in final form, ask yourself this question: "Is this as good as it has to be? Is it as good as I can make it?" Strive for excellence. Don't waste anyone's valuable time by having them critique less than your best.

Here are the people and sources that can help your career:

1. **Co-workers:** People like helping people. Chances are there is someone in your organization with marketing experience that you can build a mentor relationship with. The purpose is to gain positive feedback on projects you're working on. They may spot some pitfalls you overlooked. Or suggest a key element that's missing. Or point out areas that need polishing. The right co-worker(s) can be great sounding boards. In a way, it's like using "instant research."

2. **Outside friends:** Friends are another good source for bouncing off ideas. Ideally, you'll want one with similar interests so as to better identify with your work. If you can't get together for lunch it's amazing what information can be shared on the phone and FAX. Keep close ties with those people that can give you a reading on your ideas and projects.

3. **Suppliers:** Tap your suppliers for answers and help. Printers, for example, have the expertise to talk cutting-edge technologies in communications — from pre-press strategies to your printed piece from your computer disc. The same for other media representatives. "Partner" with them. They're good people to know.

4. **Trade Associations:** Be industry active. Trade Associations can supply you timely, useful information. Sometimes, even a proven-model for a project you may be working on. Besides helping you improve your craft, they offer a valuable networking source.

5. **Breakfast Meetings:** Successful salespeople for years have used the breakfast setting to meet with customers. Now you'll find many groups of business people sharing breakfast and ideas. So hold your own round table. With weekly or monthly sessions, you'll gain the insights you're looking for. Somehow the breakfast meeting has a magic quality that works. It is time well spent, believe me.

6. **Advertising Specialist:** Got a company milestone coming up? Or a special sales event? Or, are you going to introduce a newsletter to your dealer organization? If tight, well written professional copy is the key to the project, and there is no one internally who can do it, go outside with an advertising specialist. This will save money and wasted effort. And you may become a hero with management for bringing a new perspective to the table. They could be a free lance or retired copywriter. As the Wall Street Journal recently reported, fees for a retired specialist are modest compared to the potential payoff and benefits they offer.

Talking balloon copy draws high readership for this Sawhorse question and answer ad.

20

Ray Mithun —
An Advertising Legend

The founder of Campbell-Mithun helped put "The Land of Sky Blue Waters" on the advertising map.

Ray Mithun, founder of Campbell-Mithun

In baseball, there's Babe Ruth, Lou Gehrig, Joe DiMaggio, Ted Williams and Hank Aaron. In advertising, it's Albert Lasker, David Ogilvy, Leo Burnett, Bill Bernbach and Ray Mithun. All are well known for their high level of achievements; all made it to their industry's Hall of Fame.

Ray Mithun's agency, Campbell-Mithun, Inc., helped establish Minneapolis-St. Paul as a leading advertising center. Always the task master, Mithun motivated his agency team — including me — to make the ads "better and better." Importantly, to produce "advertising that sells."

Sky Blue Waters

One good example is "Sky Blue Waters..." for Hamms Beer. With its refreshing lake country setting, musical tom-toms and lovable bear as the Hamms icon, the campaign was the envy of the industry. (And still remembered by many consumers and studied by marketing classes.)

The advertising did more than sell beer for Hamms. It also boosted tourism for the State of Minnesota and helped boost Ray Mithun into the Advertising Hall of Fame.

"From the Land of Sky Blue Waters" was a winning theme for Hamms, a St. Paul brewery. Unlike most ad campaigns that are short lived, Hamms' "Sky Blue Waters" ran for over 15 years. (And would have probably gone longer had a conglomerate not acquired Hamms Beer and switched agencies.)

Why was the advertising so successful? Themes, slogans and umbrellas are all relatively *temporary* ad-devices. An attempt to stringing a dozen ads on a thread for the sake of consistency and a homogenous pitch to the trade and consumer. Next year, new string — new beads.

So to make it "run forever," Campbell-Mithun turned-on its "Cogwheel Power" thinking. A "Cogwheel" Idea is quite simply:

A particularly pertinent, memorable way of focusing the consumer's (and Trade) mind on the client's product or service. And that idea must be capable of efficient extension into every medium — for years to come. Power-driving everything on the account — TV, radio, newspaper, magazines, billboards, packaging and collateral material.

The timing was perfect for introducing the "lovable" Hamms Bear, an early TV icon. It was in the 1950's when TV viewers considered the commercials as special as the programming. And the animated bear was one of their favorites. The Hamms campaign, besides promoting and selling beer, showcased Campbell Mithun Advertising as a major player in the industry. (Now Campbell Mithun Esty.)

It's been years since the animated Hamms Bear has been on TV. But people still talk about him. They even remember some of his antics — how he blushed, frowned, smiled and importantly, how he "sold" Hamms Beer.

Helping Companies Pioneer

Most good agencies believe strongly in certain philosophies of their own — philosophies they try to communicate on a continuous basis throughout their organization. One such fundamental that Ray Mithun vigorously promoted was his *pioneering* philosophy. Advertising pioneering means:

- Innovating
- Originating
- Cutting new patterns
- Setting the pace

Mithun believed that the client who usually gets the most for their promotional dollar is the one who *pioneers* in one or more important facets of their marketing:

- in unique product quality
- in new products
- in product improvements
- in packaging
- in new uses for old products
- in consumer service
- in pricing
- in new methods of distribution
- in sales promotion
- in public relations
- in advertising

Technique, writing style, layout, composition, typography, etc., are important mechanics in this business. But it's the new, the original, the fresh ideas that separate great from ordinary ads.

Land O'Lakes — Creative Advertiser

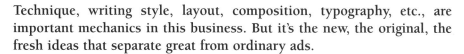

One of the best pioneering examples belongs to Land O'Lakes, an early client of Campbell-Mithun. And no one is better equipped to tell the story than Ray Mithun himself, who was a copywriter on the account.

> "As one of my first assignments, I was put to work on a butter account. (Land O'Lakes.)
>
> In those days — butter was sold and distributed in 60-pound tubs to the grocery stores in New York.
>
> When the housewife wanted butter — the grocery clerk ladled out a batch on a little wooden boat. Weighed it — along with his thumb — and wrapped it up in a piece of butcher paper.
>
> This bulk selling in unidentified consumer packages didn't provide very much opportunity for an advertising man.

But our client was a pioneer. An innovator. Against this traditional background in the trade — and despite the horrible economic conditions of the times — our client decided to introduce his product in a new sanitary, individually-wrapped, one-pound package.

Shortly thereafter — he guaranteed that all his butter was produced from cows that were tuberculin tested.

And next — he brought out butter that was churned only from sweet cream. Which was unheard of up to that time and thought to be impossible.

Then he got the government to test and certify that every pound was government graded — and made <u>only</u> from sweet cream.

I was a lucky copywriter.

I like to think that my copy was largely responsible for the phenomenal sales increases enjoyed by our client. But in my own heart — I sort of knew that the creative innovations developed by the manufacturer were the principal reasons for the continuous success of that company. I was just plain lucky to be working with such a creative advertiser."

There's a post script to this story. Campbell Mithun Esty continues to serve Ray Mithun's "creative advertiser." (Land O'Lakes joined Campbell-Mithun in 1933, the agency's first year of business.) They both must be doing something right, as the industry doesn't see that many 60-plus year client/agency relationships. Congratulations to both companies! (Both winners in their respective fields.)

An early Land O' Lakes ad written by Ray Mithun. Note how the packaging was featured — an industry first. Circa 1930's.

A Best Ever Butter Cookies ad for Land O' Lakes. (Sorry we couldn't reproduce it in 4/color, as run in Better Homes & Gardens and other leading magazines.)

Which Way Is North?

The compass is a logical symbol for marketing. It represents the principles and direction that good advertising requires. That's why Ray Mithun used the symbol to help guide his creative and account people to excellence. The agency's *"Which Way Is North?"* strategy was an effective positioning tool. It personally helped me to "hone in" on the heart of the matter in preparing good advertising.

Years later, I was pleased to see that Stephen Covey, author of "The 7 Habits of Highly Effective People," used a compass analogy in his "First Things First" seminars. During a participation session, he asked the audience to "point North." Very few people could do it. Can you?

Until you have all the facts on a product or service — *direction* — you can't prepare the proper ad. (And sadly, very little information is ever handed to you.) It is up to you to dig for facts when preparing your advertising. (Much like a reporter or detective.)

A Tribute to My Colleagues

Campbell-Mithun earned a reputation for creating "advertising that sells." (And isn't that what advertising is all about?) It was a valuable training ground for anyone that worked there. It provided the creative foundation that I needed to write this book.

Besides the great advertising, Campbell-Mithun produced *great ad people*. Some that come to mind that were influential in helping the agency grow in its middle years:

Bob Blegen	Dick Hehman	Bob Pile
George Champlin	Duane Knops	Dwight Reynolds
Dave Cloud	Jordan Krimstein	Jim Smith
Jim Cronin	Art Lund	Bill Sorem
Joe Franklin	John McGee	Dick Stevens
Dave Ganfield	Ray Mithun	Frank Walsh
Alden Grimes	Kenny Oelschlager	Al Whitman
Cleo Hovel	Gene Peterson	Dick Wilson

21

How to Advance Your Career

Invest heavily in yourself. Your talent and persistence are the most valuable assets you have.

Communications! It's the most inspiring, exciting, motivating, challenging and rewarding career possible. But don't go into it half-way. To be successful, advertising requires "blood, sweat — and ideas."

Here is some insight on how to sharpen your skills and advance your career. By following these proven, time-tested tips, you'll do your job better and reach a higher level of professional creativity.

12 Tips To The Top

1. **Sharpen the saw.** Continuing education is essential in advertising. Take in workshops and seminars to learn the trends. Read industry and related trade journals. Be a "sponge" and listen and learn from the experienced people around you. Learning is central to professional improvement. (And a responsibility to your company and yourself.)

2. **Be cross-trained** or a cross-function person. By learning and handling some of your co-workers duties, you'll be more valuable to your company. Advertising requires that you "wear a lot of hats." Wear them proudly!

3. **Stay organized.** Stay on top of your paper work and you'll make your life a whole lot easier.

4. **Be coachable.** Be willing to improve your talents through constructive criticism. This will build your performance and self-confidence.

5. **Participate in meetings.** Don't talk for the sake of talking, but be a reliable source for solid, meaningful information and ideas.

6. **Be a problem solver.** Find remedies, solutions and opportunities, not faults. Leave the complaining and "bitching" to the petty-people.

7. **Be self-disciplined.** Just do it. Do what you have to do without being pushed by your boss.

8. **Form a Mastermind Group.** For outside ideas, answers and motivation, share opinions with friends and co-workers. Networking is simply about collecting ideas, referrals and support.

9. **Have a bias for action.** To be successful, you need a sense of urgency about getting things done. Be persistent.

10. **Reach for the stars.** Never lose your pursuit for excellence. Set a standard of quality and stick to it. Always try to make your ads "better and better."

11. **Say "Yes" to a move to another city** if the opportunity arises. This will give you further experience and a new outlook to help your career grow.

12. **Use all of the innovation, energy and creativity** at your command to help reduce costs and serve your company better.

How to Make A Successful Presentation

Presentation: *"The act of presenting; descriptive or persuasive account (as by a salesman.")*

There will be many times in your business career in which you are asked to make a presentation. A presentation may take many forms and there may be more than one person involved in making it. And at any given time, there may be more than one reason for making a presentation. But you may be sure of one basic fact — a presentation is always important, and is never to be taken lightly. It is very necessary, therefore, that you understand the fundamentals of how to do a presentation well. And it is also necessary that you follow a specific procedure to make sure the points you are trying to make will come through strong and clear and effectively.

Depending on the situation, you may be called upon to make a presentation one-on-one with one person, your department superior, for example or the company CEO or someone else in top manage-

ment of your company. Or you could be asked to make a presentation to a small group, say, your company's Board of Directors or the members of a specific department, in which case you would be talking to perhaps ten or twelve people. Yet another example of a presentation situation would be where you are talking to a large group of dealers or franchisees, where the numbers could be in the hundreds or even thousands. Your preparation would vary, of course, depending on the size of the group and the specific circumstances. But the discipline you would need to follow would be fundamentally the same in each case.

The objective of a given presentation will also vary from circumstance to circumstance, but In most situations, you are trying to persuade someone in a decision-making position...to approve your recommendations. Once this person has said "Yes," you certainly will have to repeat the presentation to others who need to know what is going on, why and when and in many cases, "how much?"

In a busy, dynamic business, someone in your position may be called upon to make a presentation almost every day, two or three times a week, several times a month, frequently throughout the year. In the average advertising agency, for example, an account executive would surely make 50 or more individual presentations in a year.

So the ability to make professional, resultful presentations is critically important in virtually any kind of business. And your progress in a given job will be largely dependent on how well you perform in a given presentation.

A successful presentation can be one of the headiest experiences in business. Getting approval of your plan can make your day. In many businesses, a person who can make truly great presentations is very likely to one day occupy the top spot in the company.

Summing up, there are many people in business who can make a fairly good presentation. But there are relatively few who can make a *truly great* presentation, and do it again and again to any kind of audience. And to come at it from the opposite point of view, people who make poor presentations seldom rise into top management.

Making an effective presentation calls for a combination of instinct, organization, knowledge of the subject, salesmanship and finally, the ability to follow a disciplined procedure.

A Few Examples of Situations Calling for a Presentation

1. To get approval of your recommendations from the CEO of your company.

2. To give the members of a department a look at a plan that has been given previous approval.

3. To inform and motivate a large group of (for example) dealers who handle your company's products.

4. To get approval of your plans and recommendations from a Dealer Group or Franchisee Council.

5. To inform a management group of an entirely new idea or venture you wish the company to undertake.

In each case, your presentation is a logical step in a situation where eventually *something is going to happen.*

A Presentation Can Take Many Forms

1. One on one with your boss or company CEO or executive.

2. You presenting to several people.

3. You presenting to a large group.

In each case you must evaluate what you need to do a good job.

1. Will you need visual materials? If so, what kind?

   ...Charts?

   ...Graphs?

   ...Pictures?

   ...Ad layouts?

2. How much time have you got to get ready?

   ...An hour?

   ...A couple of days?

   ...A couple of weeks or months?

3. Where will the presentation take place?

   ...Boss's office?

   ...Company Board Room?

...Hotel conference room?

...Hotel grand ballroom?

...Dealer's lunch room?

...Another city?

4. How much time will you be given?

...Fifteen minutes?

...An hour?

...Not determined?

5. Will you need help?

...Audio/visual people?

...Someone to operate whatever equipment needed?

...An assistant of some kind?

Some "Do's" and "Don'ts" in Making Your Presentation

Note: These are a few simple rules which have been tested and proved in literally thousands of presentations. Not all apply to each situation, but most of them do.

1. Don't start your presentation with a joke.

2. Don't ever apologize by saying: "I don't know why I'm up here. I'm not an expert." (In the eyes of the audience, you are.)

3. Don't have too many presenters. Two or three at most. One is almost always better.

4. Don't use jargon.

5. Don't stand in front of your overhead projector.

6. Don't throw used materials on the floor.

7. Don't wear clothes unsuitable to the atmosphere of the meeting.

8. Don't ever make a presentation in a room with which you are not familiar. Check it out in advance.

On the other hand......

1. Do make a check list and follow it precisely.

2. Do have a focus. A high point. Build on it and away from it.

3. Do have an overall presentation strategy. Put it in writing for your own constant reference.

4. Do know how much time you will have and how long each part/section will take.

5. Do be prepared for surprises.

6. Do anticipate questions.

7. Do answer questions precisely and do say "I don't know" if you don't know. If you can't answer a question in a couple of sentences or so, don't try.

8. Do know in advance that no matter what period of time you think it will take for you to make your presentation, the ACTUAL PRE-SENTATION WILL ALWAYS TAKE LONGER.

9. Do rehearse! Rehearse! Rehearse!

A Final Comment

Some people are natural-born presenters. Some are not and have to work at it. But both kinds will do a better job if they prepare, follow a tough-minded discipline. No one is so darned good that they can depend on their natural talent to get through. It takes time, it takes work, it takes thorough preparation to do a fine job. Even the most talented, instinctive presenter becomes helpless if his equipment fails or the room is not big enough or his visual material cannot be seen and his voice becomes lost to those in the back of the room.

Remember this: If a presenter starts out by saying, "Can you all hear me in the back of the room?" Or "Is this mike working?" Or "Can you all see this chart?".... that presenter is almost sure to fail.

The best presenters *know* their material can be seen in the back of the room, they *know* their voice can be heard and they have rehearsed the living daylights out of what they are going to say and do.

Summing up....

A successful presentation
made by you is like
winning the Super Bowl!

Where the Jobs Are

Good news! Communications rank high in the top growth industries for
the 21st Century. Here's the job listing as compiled by the leading executive search firms.

1. High-tech

2. Health Care

3. Medical/pharmaceutical

4. **Communications**

5. Environmental

6. Financial Services

7. Manufacturing

8. Consumer Products

9. Electronics

*Be cross trained so you
can wear lots of hats. . .
and be more valuable.*

kinko's résumés

Résumé Guide

30 Seconds Is All You Get!

This is the average time a manager takes to scan a résumé and determine if the applicant should be granted an interview. It's true—you may have spent thousands of dollars on your education and training, and all you have now is just 30 seconds to sell yourself to a prospective employer.

For this reason, it is essential the materials you use to market yourself project a professional image. Your résumé and cover letter not only need to be targeted to the specific type of industry and business you're trying to enter, they must also present a style and feel which encourages the reader to take a closer look.

Kinko's Copy Centers offer everything you need to launch an effective job search: Kinko's Résumés (our document creation service), self-service Macintosh® computers, résumé paper, high quality copies, matching envelopes, and this Résumé Guide. Kinko's is ready to serve as your job search support center.

When every second counts, you can depend on Kinko's for expert résumé assistance and friendly, personal care.

The Importance of Résumé Paper

Because your résumé serves as your first introduction to a prospective employer, it needs to present a quality, professional image. This is why the color and quality of the résumé paper you choose is so important.

Kinko's résumé paper ensures that you make a strong and distinctive first impression. We offer an excellent array of résumé materials:

- high quality 24-pound paper
- sophisticated color selections suitable to a wide range of fields
- matching business-size envelopes
- white catalog envelopes so you can send your résumé and cover letter unfolded.

Ten Tips For Designing A Successful Résumé

Keep the following suggestions in mind when developing your résumé and cover letter:

★ Know your audience—use the vocabulary and speak the language of your targeted field.

★ Write your job objective from the standpoint of what you can offer your prospective employer and company.

★ Describe your experiences from an accomplishment point-of-view.

★ Present all information positively: if anything could possibly be interpreted negatively, either don't use it, or rewrite it with a positive perspective. Be honest, but don't present an easy reason to eliminate you from consideration.

★ Utilize strong, active words for emphasis. For example:
Action verbs:
achieved, expedited, managed, produced, created, directed, initiated.
Positive modifiers:
actively, substantially, effectively, efficiently, quickly.

★ Make your résumé easy to read or scan. Leave plenty of open space. Eliminate all typos! Use a layout and lettering that allows easy viewing.

★ Test your résumé for relevancy — all information should directly support your job objective or work abilities. If it doesn't, leave it out.

★ Develop and maintain a list of references, and have it available upon request. Don't include it in mailings.

★ Make sure that the information in your cover letter (employer name, title, address, position applied for) is accurate.

★ Keep it short! The longer your résumé is, the less it will be read.

© Kinko's of Minnesota, 1997

Better than money, the answers, ideas and motivation you can get from viable suppliers, like Kinko's.

22

Win-Win With Suppliers

Improve your advertising performance with a closer relationship with printers, media representatives and all suppliers.

Long before "win-win" became a buzzword, Frank Sinatra was living it. During his recording sessions he inspired the musicians to play to their full potential. This helped produce some of the greatest music tracks ever recorded. And this, in turn, helped drive Sinatra to richer performances himself. A perfect win-win arrangement.

Marketing suppliers, akin to musicians, can perform better for you and your organization if you let them. Even with challenging assignments and demanding deadlines, they can perform their full potential, also. Likewise, they can also produce mediocre jobs, if you allow them. As a professional, it is up to you to lead suppliers — i.e., ad specialist, printer, radio station, etc. — to the high standards you set and require. (As Sinatra did.)

Getting the most "bang" from all your outside resources requires that you work closely with them on a "partnership" basis. Most innovative organizations include them in their "win-win" agreements, as below:

Win-Win contract between:

- Employees
- Customers
- Stockholders
- Suppliers

Advantages of "Partnerships"

Building long term relationships with your marketing suppliers can be beneficial to your company. First of all, they'll become familiar with your account and your way of doing business. As a frequent customer with them you'll be in a better position to request "rush" jobs when necessary. Also, you'll have earned priority if and when shortages occur. Lastly, you'll have established a credit record that is more important than ever today.

Suppliers on a "partnership" basis will go the extra mile to keep your business. They'll show you ways to be more cost-efficient. (They want *you* to win, also.) A smart supplier will recommend alternatives if their product is not appropriate for you. They know your future business is valuable and that you'll return to them when the fit is right.

> *Example:* A small black and white press run of 500 at a full service 4/color printer could be costly. Likewise, so could a 5,000 run at a photo copy center. A good printer will point this out, even if it costs them the job.

Spelling-Out the Job

One simple way to avoid cost over-runs in advertising is by spelling out the job. Too many times faulty instructions require the supplier to re-do parts of a job. (At your expense.) Take the extra time and prepare a job outline with specific instructions. Also, hold face-to-face production meetings to review the job with suppliers.

About the Low Bidder

Would you hire the low bid person to pack your parachute? Not every advertiser goes with the low bid. You may pay more in the long run through:

• Hidden costs

• Missed deadline

• An unsatisfactory job

No one remembers how "cheap" a job was; only how bad it was. My experience has taught me that there is no "free" lunch. So, weigh your options carefully when reviewing bids and picking a supplier.

How to Pick Suppliers

Factors to consider when selecting a supplier for your marketing activities:

- Delivery capabilities

- Quality

- Price

- Technical ability

- Performance

- Help and advice

Before going with a supplier, talk to two or three of their customers. Competent suppliers are proud to share testimonials.

Negotiating with Suppliers

Large corporations, because of their buying power, expect to get the best prices from their vendors. And they usually do. Volume leveraging and purchasing power are an intrinsic part of our business system. But that doesn't mean that you, as a small or midsized company, can't get good buys also. They're often available. But you have to ask for them.

Basic Supplier Tips

1. **Negotiate at the beginning**. You'll always have more bargaining power before any contract or purchase order is signed.

2. **Get at least three bids on major jobs** from printers and graphic houses.

3. **Inquire about discounts** that may be pending. (i.e., Volume, new customer or pre-pay discounts.)

4. **If no discounts apply**, ask for an extra 30 days to pay. Quite often you'll get it.

5. **Promotional allowances**. Quite common in the food industry, perhaps your vendor will be creative and find a way to pass on some kind of a promotional allowance to get or keep your business.

6. **Consider a "vendor's option" buy**. Often, printers, sign makers, graphic houses and other suppliers have "dead time." They'll accept jobs at reduced costs when done on their terms. By planning ahead you may find a good deal.

7. **Don't over spec a job**. Too often advertisers are too specific when working with printers. By using material on hand, you can usually save money. The U.S. Government pays $200 for hammers because they "over-spec" the job.

8. **Ask about "un-sold" spots** that a radio or TV station can offer. They may fall late at night, but if you can be flexible, you'll get some great buys.

9. **Get a radio jingle buy-out**. Otherwise you could be paying talent re-use fees for a long time to come. Inquire about a talent buy-out before the jingle is produced.

10. **Use colored paper stock** instead of 2/color on routine mailings. You'll get almost the same attention and impact. And reduce printing costs. Have your printer show the wide variety of "hot" colors he/she stocks.

11. **Before starting a brochure**, ask your printer what paper they recommend. They may have some left-over stock that will cost less than using custom paper that has to be special-ordered. Also be sure your layout conforms to the paper size. On a long press run you'll save money by using less paper.

12. **Take time to spell-out the job** with every supplier. Make sure the communications line is open. By starting off the job right — with detailed instructions — you'll avoid mistakes, and possibly, some costly "re-do's."

13. **Hold supplier reviews**. Extra costs can leak in over time that may be more than inflation. When necessary, do some "creative shopping" and seek out quality suppliers who meet your standards — and offer competitive prices.

ALWAYS
SPELL
OUT
THE JOB!

23

The Top 25 Resources

A book bonus! Here's the author's pick for the first team in media and marketing support.

Selecting the right media and marketing suppliers is essential for cost-effective advertising. But it isn't necessarily the "low bidder" that's the best choice. Sub-standard printing for your company brochure, for example, can hurt your image. Or, if your radio commercials are not reaching the right audience, you're losing money.

As you know, marketing resources — from printers to premium people — are plentiful. The same for media selection. But which ones to use? To lend a helping hand, here are 25 areas of marketing communications support. As you'll see, some categories have several companies listed, as each may have a specific niche. Here is my choice for the Top 25 Resources. They're good! Give them a try.

1. Desktop Publishing

- Icon Productions, Inc. - Minneapolis, MN (612) 871-1233

- PBS Graphic Art & Design - Richfield, MN (612) 866-8159

- Kinko's Copy Center - Edina, MN (612) 820-6000

2. Advertising Agencies

- Campbell Mithun Esty - Minneapolis, MN (612) 347-1000

- Colle & McVoy - Bloomington, MN (612) 897-7500

- Gordon Robinson & Asso. - Minneapolis, MN (612) 831-4666

- Miller Meester - Minneapolis, MN (612) 337-6600

3. Freelance Copywriter (Advertising Specialist)

- Sandy Bucholtz - Minneapolis, MN (612) 823-2904

- Bob Volden - St. Paul, MN (612) 647-9078

4. Public Relations

- Jackson Communications, Inc. - Edina, MN (612) 941-0743

- Shandwick - Bloomington, MN (612) 831-8515

- Koopman Marketing Communications - Minneapolis, MN (612) 881-0261

5. Printers

A. *Fast Copy and Do-It-Yourself Computer Center*

- Kinko's Copy Center - Edina, MN (612) 820-6000

B. *Off-Set (Includes 2/color)*

- The Printmakers - New Hope, MN (612) 542-8707

- Racy Printing - St. Paul, MN (612) 641-0955

C. *Full Service (Includes 4/color)*

- Ideal Printers, Inc. - St. Paul, MN (612) 646-0133

- John Roberts Co. - Minneapolis, MN (612) 755-5500

- Anderberg-Lund Printing - Minneapolis, MN (800) 231-9777

D. *Short Run Color Printing*

- Digital Impressions - Shoreview, MN (800) 263-0823

E. *Web Offset (Advertising Supplements)*

- Shakopee Valley Printing - Shakopee, MN (612) 445-8260

6. Electronic Graphics and Litho Prep

- A.S.A.P., Inc. - Minneapolis, MN (612) 926-4735

7. Photo Copies and Finishing

- Photo's Inc. - Minneapolis, MN (612) 721-2601

8. **Stock Photos & Video**

   • Charlton Photos, Inc. - Mequon, WI (414) 241-8634

9. **Photography**

   A. *Studio*

      • Drew Trampe Photography - Minneapolis, MN (612) 379-1924

   B. *Location Shooting*

      • Cheryl Walsh Bellville Photography - St. Paul, MN (612) 291-8483

10. **Signs**

    • H&W Specialties - St. Paul, MN (612) 639-0559 (Includes silk screen process)

    • Sign-A-Rama, USA - Bloomington, MN (612) 881-2799

    • Sign Design, Inc. - St. Paul, MN (612) 290-2212

11. **Displays and Graphics**

    • Skyline Displays Midwest - Burnsville, MN (612) 895-6000; (800) 328-2725

    • The Graphix Shop - Bloomington, MN (612) 683-9665

    • PBS Graphic Art & Design - Richfield, MN (612) 866-8159

12. **Promotional Products (Ad Specialties)**

    • Westco Recognition Advertising - St. Louis Park, MN (612) 926-7718

    • Lonergan Advertising - Minneapolis, MN (612) 944-7228

    • K-Products, Inc. - Orange City, IA (800) 369-2277

13. **Employee/Customer Awards & Recognition**

    • James & Company - South St. Paul, MN (612) 451-3850

    • BI Performance Services - Minneapolis, MN (612) 835-4800

14. **Training & Learning Center**

    • Wilson Learning - Eden Prairie, MN (612) 944-3150

15. **Radio Stations (Minneapolis-St. Paul Market)**

   • WCCO (830 AM) - News/Talk/Sports; (612) 370-0611

   • KQRS (92.5 FM) - Rock; (612) 545-5601

   • KDWB (101.3 FM) - Pop; (612) 340-9000

   • KEEY (102.1 FM) - Country; (612) 820-4200

   • WLTE (102.9 FM) - Easy listening; (612) 339-1029

   • KSTP (94.5 FM) - Contemporary; (612) 642-4141

   • KSTP (1500 AM) - Talk; (612) 481-9333

   • KQQL (107.9 FM) - Oldies; (612) 338-8118

   • KEGE (93.7 FM) - Alternative; (612) 545-5601

   • WBOB (100.3 FM) - Hard rock; (612) 338-8118

   • KLBB (1400/1470 AM) - Big band/nostalgia; (612) 341-1720

16. **Music Arrangers (Radio Jingles/TV Tracks)**

   • Hest Kramer - Edina, MN (612) 831-3266

   • Saxe Productions - Appleton, WI (414) 730-0300

17. **Talent & Talent Agencies (Announcers)**

   • Sound Alternatives & A.C.T.V. - St. Paul, MN (612) 454-0150

   • N.U.T.S. (Non-Union -Talent-Service) - (612) 544-9450

   • Ms. Sandy Bucholtz - Minneapolis, MN (612) 823-2904

18. **TV Stations (Minneapolis - St. Paul Market)**

   • Fox 29 WFTC - (612) 379-2929

   • KARE 11; NBC - (612) 546-1111

   • KMSP 9; Independent - (612) 944-9999

   • KSTP 5; ABC - (612) 646-5555

   • WCCO 4; CBS - (612) 339-4444

   • Paragon Cable - (612) 522-2000

19. **Recording Services (Sound & Video)**

   • Greatapes - Minneapolis, MN (612) 872-8284

   • CME Video & Film - Minneapolis, MN (612) 347-1700

   • Hudson-Forrester Studios, Inc. - Edina, MN - (612) 835-9952

20. **Audio/Visual Rental Services**

   • Blumberg Communications, Inc. - Minneapolis, MN (612) 521-8225

21. **Coupon and Rebate Fulfillment Services**

   • FSI Fulfillment Systems, Inc. - Monticello, MN (612) 295-3400

22. **Internet Services**

   • MRNet - (612) 362-5800

   • Web Business Register - (310) 545-8864

23. **Direct Mail Services**

   • ALDATA - Apple Valley, MN (612) 432-6900

   • Braemar Mailing Service - Edina, MN (612) 828-9755

   • Polk Company - (800) 637-7655

   • American Sales Leads - Minneapolis, MN (612) 897-1033

   • Midwest Direct Marketing Association - Minneapolis, MN (612) 927-9220

24. **Outdoor Advertising**

   • Universal Outdoor, Inc. - Richfield, MN (612) 869-1900

   • 3M Media - (800) 759-3838

   • Collins Outdoor Advertising, Inc. - LaCrosse, WI (608) 784-8200; (800) 658-9095

25. **Buttons & Badges**

   • Wendell's - Ramsey, MN (612) 576-8200; (800) 328-3692

Remarks: For additional marketing communications suppliers, call the author, Dick Hill, at (612) 941-3837.

SOME OF OUR GRADUATES STUDIED UNDER FIRE.

OFFICIAL U.S. MARINE CORPS PHOTO

Dick Hill, class of '67, receives combat award for his radio reporting from Korea.

Before completing his studies at the University of Minnesota, Dick Hill left to serve with the U.S. Marines in Korea. Stationed with the First Marine Division, Sgt. Hill was decorated for his front line radio broadcasts heard by millions over the ABC, CBS and NBC networks.

Assigned to the Public Information Office (P.I.O.), Hill was a radio correspondent during some of the heaviest fighting in the Communist Chinese sector. Without regard for his own personal safety, Hill distinguished himself with his series.

"A Message from A Marine."

His reporting became some of the "homework" and real life experience that helped him excel in both radio and journalism when he returned to the U. of M.

Today, he is still involved in broadcast through his position as V.P. marketing, The Farm-Oyl company, St. Paul. He actively promotes the University as a member of the National Agricultural Marketing Association (NAMA). He has also served on the Alumni Task Force Committee.

THE UNIVERSITY OF MINNESOTA ALUMNI ASSOCIATION

Here's a well designed layout. The photo creates the motivation to read the copy. (The author was featured in this ad; part of a series for the University of Minnesota.)

24

Common Terms (Glossary)

Every industry has its own buzz words. Here's the language you'll be speaking your entire career.

To help you excel in today's high-tech world of marketing communications, here are many of the words and common terms you'll be using. They apply to all areas of the industry, including:

- Marketing
- Advertising
- Sales Promotion
- Merchandising
- Retailing
- Printing
- Media

A

ad slick, reproduction *line art* supplied by marketer to retailer for use in local *ROP* or circular advertising. Usually on a glossy paper stock.

advertising, the use of paid media to generate awareness of a product or service, establish an image, and stimulate purchase intention.

advertising allowance, payment by national marketer to retailer, intended to reimburse that retailer for local advertising of marketer's product.

advertising specialty, product used as *giveaway* to stimulate corporate remembrance, usually *imprinted* with company name/address/phone number.

agate line, Unit of print media space measurement, 1 column wide x 1/14 inch deep. (Thus, 14 agate lines = 1 *column inch..*)

agency commission, revenue generated by an agency, based upon a % override to the cost of program production or media placement. Also, in advertising, the commission paid by media to agency, typically 15%.

airbrush, graphic technique in which ink is applied with compressed air, similar to spray painting, to render a soft, airy effect. Frequently used in *retouching*.

allowance, discount offered by a marketer to *retailer* or *wholesaler*, usually in return for a specific performance; i.e., stocking, buying, paying cash, merchandising, et al.

antitrust, term referring to illegal actions taken by a business to effectively prevent competition. (See *Sherman Antitrust Law, Robinson-Patman Act..*)

art, in marketing, a photo or illustration intended for reproduction.

audience, in *media*, a measurement referring to the number of *households* watching a given program segment. (See *rating.*)

audio-visual aids, buzzword for the entire category of materials/techniques utilized to help a speaker support his/her presentation.

awareness, consumer's recall of information about a brand or ad.

B

bait & switch, unethical retail practice of advertising an unusually low-priced item, often not even available, to lure shoppers to a retail store, where they can be sold a higher-priced item.

banner, *point-of-sale*, usually a rectangle of plastic or cloth, with grommets in the corners, designed to be suspended from ceilings or posts.

bar code, a pattern of stripes on printed material, which can be read by laser beam, and translated to identification numbers. Example: the *UPC* code on packaging.

barter, trading of products (often leftovers) by a marketer, in return for receiving media or promotion properties. Usually handled by a "barter agent/broker."

bells & whistles, slang for promotional "spins" or extra features *overlayed* for the purpose of attracting attention.

benday, in printing, a process that achieves the effects of *half-tones* without half-tone work, usually accomplished by overlaying patterned plastic sheets atop *line art*. The patterns are measured by the percentage of art they displace; e.g., a 10% benday blocks out 10% of original art.

billboard, popular name for outdoor advertising signage. Also, in television, a presentation of the name and/or slogan of the sponsor, at the start/close of a program. Usually 8 seconds in length.

billing rate, (hourly rate), fee established for each agency person who works on client's business. Usually a multiple of that employee's compensation, to cover overhead/fringes/profit.

bingo card, reader-reply card, inserted near the back of a publication, featuring many numbers which can be circled by readers to receive additional information from advertisers in that periodical.

black & white, usually refers to photographic art without color or a publication that is printed with no color; i.e., black ink on white paper.

bleed, a printing area extended (or "bled") to the boundaries of the final sheet, thereby eliminating any white margin border.

blue line, the line drawn in blue ink on *mechanical art,* which indicates where *die-cutting* will occur. It is blue so that the black-and-white camera won't record it.

blueprint, photographic contact print, usually used to check/confirm layout and imposition of *mechanical art* prior to plate-making.

body copy, (See text), the words in an ad which support/amplify the *headlines* and *subheads.*

bold face, a darker/heavier version of a type style or *font.* Commonly used in headlines or wherever emphasis is desired.

bonus goods, type of *allowance,* in which a marketer ships extra salable goods to a retailer - as a quantity-purchase incentive.

bonus pack, special packaging that provides consumer with extra quantity of merchandise at no extra cost over "regular" pack. For example: "1/3 More Free."

bounce-back, additional promotion offer made to respondents of an initial offer, usually intended to encourage *repeat purchase* or *continuity.*

box-top offer, an incentive offer (usually consumer-oriented) for a premium item which is based on the return of one-or-more "box-tops" as *proof-of-purchase.*

brand loyalty, advertising buzzword for the outdated theory that consumers are "loyal" to a particular brand. It is now generally believed that modern consumers have a mental "menu of acceptable brands."

brand-switcher, consumer who exhibits little or no *brand loyalty.*

brochure, any booklet of 4 or more pages, promoting a product/service.

bulk mail, second-class, third-class and fourth-class mail, serviced on a non-preferential basis by the United States Post Office.

bulk mailing, large number of identical pieces, delivered together to the Post Office, to qualify for reduced "third-class" rate.

C

CPM, (Cost Per Thousand), relative measure of media cost. Total cost of an ad, divided by the potential audience reached, usually expressed in thousands of persons or *households.*

calligraphy, fine hand-lettering. "Calligraphic" type resembles penmanship.

camera-ready, mechanical art completely ready, without further alteration, for the printing process - the first step of which is "the camera," used for photographically producing film (or today, a *scanner* for electronic production.)

campaign, coordinated advertising and promotion effort, intended to continue thematically over time.

canvass, visitation of retail or wholesale customers in a given market, to learn about sales situation, competitive activity, opportunities, etc.

card rate, the published rate for a communications medium, prior to any discounts.

caret, editor's mark (^) to indicate where corrections or additions are to be inserted in *copy*.

caricature, *illustration* of a person which features deliberate exaggeration, to achieve humor.

carriage trade, term to describe affluent, "upscale" consumers.

cash refund, offer by marketer to consumer to refund money in return for submission of *proof-of-purchase* affidavits.

catalog house, retailer who publishes a catalog, from which shoppers order at a customer-service desk, waiting for merchandise to be brought out from the back-room warehouse. Presented as cost-saving shopping, based on reduced personnel/overhead.

cents-off, discount from marketer to consumer, usually delivered as actual reduced price or "cents-off," on specially-marked product.

chain, group of *retailers*, centrally owned and operated.

Chromacom, *trademarked* name of a highly sophisticated computer-driven *color separation* laser scanner capable of electronic retouching and stripping.

chrome, a color *transparency*, with a positive photographic image, produced on film.

circular, usually refers to newsprint price feature piece "circulated" by a retailer to its local market customer base.

clearing house, a business that receives/counts/relays *coupons* and *rebates*, and forwards them to manufacturers for payment.

clip art, existing art, as opposed to specially-commissioned, which is "clipped" from a book or electronic file, and re-used as reproduction art.

cold-call, in selling, to approach a prospect via telephone or in person with no prior introduction or request.

collate, a *bindery* operation - to gather together, in sequence, elements which comprise a complete set.

collateral, any and all printed material intended to support a brand promotional effort.

color bars, printed designations on *four-color process* proofs which show ink densities used, as a guide to making corrections.

color break, indications on black and white *mechanical art*, specifying colors which are to be printed.

color key, (See *progressives*), photographic representation of each of four *color separation* printers transferred to clear acetate to show values of individual colors as well as in combination. Not usually to prove reproduction quality, but as more elaborate version of *blueprint*. If laminated together, usually referred to as *transfer print.*.

color separation, the separation of multi-colored original art by camera or laser scan techniques, to produce individual, separated colors. Usually as four separations: *yellow, magenta* (red), *cyan* (blue) plus black, for full-color printing.

color swatch, a small patch of solid color, pasted to *mechanical art*, as a printer's guide to match the final color desired.

column inch, unit of newspaper/magazine space; 1 column wide x 1 inch deep. (14 *agate lines*.)

co-marketing, jointly-designed partnership *marketing* between manufacturers/brand and retailers.

comprehensive, *(comp)*, in art, a presentation sketch that represents what will be the finished piece.

computer graphics, electronic imaging; art activated by electronic means.

computer personalization, the utilization of computer technology to make *direct mail* pieces individualized, through the use of names, phrases, addresses, etc.

computer typesetting, setting type electronically, as opposed to mechanically.

consignment, *retailer* takes possession of goods, but does not have to pay until he sells them. Can return unsold goods to *marketer*.

consumer, generally, the ultimate purchaser of a product or service. Sometimes called: "customer," "shopper," "patron," "buyer."

continuous tone, any piece of artwork comprised of tonal effects which requires it to be *screened* into *dots* for reproduction. The result will be a *half-tone*.

coop advertising, advertising run by local retailer featuring the product of a national manufacturer. Usually on a shared-cost, "co-operative" basis.

copy, in *marketing*, the words that accompany a visual and amplify the *headline*. Also: the *text*..

copy platform, a statement of the basic idea(s) that the advertising message is intended to convey, to gain client approval prior to releasing the project to creative development.

coupon, store-redeemable piece of printed paper, with stated monetary value, that a shopper can redeem immediately for savings by presenting to a retailer at the time of purchase of the item.

creative, general description of the activity related to the development of promotion materials. Includes concepts, design, *copy*.

crop, removing (at the camera stage) those areas of a photograph or other original, not required to be printed. Also: indicating the unwanted areas of a photo/illustration.

cut-and-paste, to edit a manuscript by physically or electronically, cutting elements apart and re-arranging them.

cyberspace, a realistic simulation of an environment, including 3-dimensional graphics, by a computer system using interactive software and hardware.

D

Day-Glo, *trademark* for printing inks permeated with a fluorescent substance, which creates a bright "glow" effect, used primarily in outdoor printing. Occasionally used for special effects on in-store displays.

dealer incentive, reward given to a retailer, in return for promotional support for quantity purchase.

dealer listing, portion of marketer's advertisement devoted to listing local retailers who carry that marketer's product(s).

dealer loader, incentive given to wholesaler or retailer in return for quantity purchase. Often, a premium fastened to *point-of-sale* display, to make sure that display is noticed by a retail manager.

desk-top publishing, term coined by Aldus PageMaker®, describing the ability of microcomputer software and hardware to enable an operator to control graphics, text, page design and production from a single work station.

direct mail, unsolicited promotional material delivered to consumers by *bulk mail.* Unaffectionately referred to as "junk mail."

direct response, *marketing* directly to consumers by mail, catalog or other home delivery, attempting to solicit orders by mail or toll-free telephone.

display, arrangement of product, usually accompanied by printed signage, placed to attract shopper attention in a retail store.

display advertising, printed advertising that includes illustration in addition to *type.*

door-opener, premium designed to motivate prospect to listen to sales pitch.

double-truck, industry term for a two-page ad. Also: a "spread."

drive time, in radio, time periods during which people commute. Varies by market, but generally considered to be 6-10 AM and 3-7 PM, Monday through Friday.

drop shadow, graphic device in which *type* or other element, is reproduced with an offset second image on one edge, giving a "shadow" effect which visually "lifts" the primary *type,* and makes the image appear 3-dimensional.

dub, in film making, to electronically substitute a sound or voice for the one actually recorded live. Often, the means of providing audio translations of "foreign" soundtracks.

dummy, a bland, three-dimensional make-up as a simulation of the job to be printed.

E

ECR, (Efficient Consumer Response), buzz-phrase referring to the desire and attempt by grocery marketers to eliminate the inherently inefficient parts of the system of creating, selling and distributing products.

E-Mail, computer communications system that permits users to send desk-top messages/files to one another.

eighty/twenty rule, the "heavy-user/heavy-seller" theory, which says that 20% of consumers buy 80% of your product, 20% of retailers sell 80%, etc. Usually remarkably accurate.

embossing, same as *debossing,* except the image is raised, as opposed to depressed.

event marketing, a themed activity taking place "live"; e.g., car race, state fair, sporting event, concert, etc., related to the selling of a product or group of products.

F

FCC, (Federal Commerce Commission), regulatory agency whose decisions influence various promotional techniques, for example, *sweepstakes* rules. (202) 632-7000.

FOB, (Free On Board or Freight On Board), goods are quoted including delivery to a specified shipping point. Buyer incurs any additional costs to move those goods to their final destination(s).

FSI, (Free-Standing Insert), an advertisement, printed separately, and inserted into newspapers. Usually full-color, and most often used in Sunday editions. Several companies are in the business of selling fractional-space units in multi-page FSI's. Frequently used medium for couponing and promotional offers.

FTC, (Federal Trade Commission), Federal regulatory agency, which oversees fair trade practices, including enforcing *Robinson-Patman* Act. (202) 326-2222.

face value, the redeemable value of a *coupon*.

facings, the total number of package fronts visible on a retail shelf, in one linear row. Two packages stacked vertically are "one facing."

factory outlet, retail store operated by the marketer of a line of merchandise.

fall-off, in art, a graduation from dark to light, commonly used as a background to create illusion of depth.

farm out, work not produced directly by an agency, rather sub-contracted out to vendors and/or freelancers.

fax, (facsimile transfer), indispensable communications device enabling agency to communicate with distant client by transmitting written "hardcopy" documents over telephone lines.

feature, promotional effort for a product, provided by retailer, usually in the form of *display*, price reduction or *co-op advertising*.

film, in printing, the photographic materials that contain the desired image. Printing *plates* are then made from the *film*.

fine print, manuscript copy of very small type size, intentionally difficult to read because it is legalistic in nature or irrelevant to the point of the piece.

finishing, to *die-cut*, fold, assemble or otherwise complete the process of manufacturing a printed brochure, booklet or display. Includes packing and *making ready* to ship.

first generation, a copy of *artwork* made from the original. Generally required for quality *reproduction*. When copies are made from copies, they become "second" or "third" generations, etc., with corresponding loss in faithfulness to the master.

flag, interruptive graphic device on a package that announces or "flags," a promotional offer.

flat color, the used of specified matched colors, printed in a solid value, to achieve a graphic effect. As opposed to *process* color.

flip chart, sales presentation comprised of several pages of bullet points, designed to stand on a buyer's desk and serve as an aid to the salesperson.

flow chart, simplified *PERT* chart, laying out the steps of a project in chronological order by critical decision-making due dates.

flush, lines of type that align to a vertical margin. *Flush left* refers to left margin of page. *Flush right* refers to the right margin of the page.

flyer, (flier), inexpensive, 1-page (usually 8-1/2" x 11") promotional sheet, typically intended for handout or *bulk mailing*.

Fome-Cor, Monsanto *trademark* for a type of *board* made of polystyrene foam compressed flat and laminated on two dies with "solid bleached sulfate" tag. Extremely rigid, yet light in weight. Ideal for *embossing/debossing* effects.

font, a complete set of characters, numerals and punctuation in a given *typeface/size.*

form, a printed unit consisting of one side of paper stock which may contain one or more images/pages.

form letter, a "stock" communiqué sent to multiple recipients, unchanged except for salutation.

four-color process, printing a photographic or multi-colored image with the primary colors: *yellow, magenta, cyan* (blue), and *black,* for full-color reproduction. As opposed to *flat color* printing.

free, one of the most powerful words in promotion. But if used without stipulation, *FTC* regulations require that the offer be "totally without cost or consideration."

freelance, to do work for an agency as an independent contractor, rather than as an employee.

frequency, in *media* terms, the number of times a defined *target audience* is exposed to an ad or promotional message.

frequent-user program, a *continuity* program which provides consumer awards, usually based upon registering and continuing to purchase. The most famous of these events is the "frequent flyer" program.

G

GRP, (Gross Rating Point), in *media,* the sum total of the *ratings* for an advertising schedule, usually stated by week. Theoretically, 100 GRP's could either mean 100% of households are reached once per week.

gatefold, an oversize page that folds into the *gutter,* often used to extend the size of an advertisement in a magazine or a map in a book; e.g., the Playboy "centerfold." A smaller brochure can also be *gatefolded.*

gazebo, a *point-of-sale* island display fixture, generally free-standing, which can be shopped from 360°, i.e., from all sides.

generics, unbranded consumer products, in plain (usually white) packaging, sold at substantially lower prices than advertised brands.

gift-with-purchase, promotion technique, most frequently seen in department stores, in which shopper is rewarded with an on-the-spot *premium*; i.e., "buy a fragrance set, get a make-up bag, free."

glossy, photo with a shiny, hard finish. As opposed to *matte,* which is nonreflective.

gondola, a section of shelving in a retail store.

gothic, style of *typeface.* Block letters without decoration, as opposed to *serif* faces, which have finishing strokes. Also: *sans serif.*

grain, in papermaking, the direction of the fibers. An important consideration in terms of *warpage.*

gripper edge, the edge of a paper sheet which is unprintable, because it is needed to allow the mechanical "grippers" to pick and carry the sheet through the printing or *die-cutting* process.

grommet, a metal-protected hole, punched into *board* or *banner* . Used to receive threaded rope or wire for hanging purposes.

H

HBA, designation for the "Health and Beauty Aids" section of a grocery store.

HH, (Households), abbreviation for the definition of a living unit. Many modified definitions include: "single-family HH," "multi-family HH," "female-headed HH," et al.

handbill, printed *flyer* that is literally "handed out" in public places.

handling allowance, incentive from marketer to trade to "handle" (stock) a product or an extra incentive for stocking an item that requires special handling. Also, the fee paid to retailers for "handling" *coupons.*

hard sell, forceful approach to persuasion, usually involving basic "gut" emotional appeals, including: this is your "last chance."

hardware, generic term for physical computing equipment, as opposed to *software,* which refers to programs necessary to make hardware useful.

hickie, in printing, a defect/spot in a solid area caused by dust or dried ink particle.

hitchhike, literally, a "free ride." A marketer includes an offer within the vehicle of another, to reach the same *target audience* at no cost.

home-video shopping, direct-to-consumer selling technique, wherein product offerings are exposed over a *cable TV* channel, and prospects order by dialing toll-free phone number, using credit card to pay.

hot-button, any marketing technique capable of triggering an immediate consumer response.

house account, a customer reserved for, and serviced by, company management — as opposed to being assigned to a sales rep.

house organ, publication produced internally by a company, with controlled circulation.

I

IBM Coupon, industry term for a small *coupon,* of standard size 3-1/2" x 2-3/16". Usually the smallest size a *client* or *medium* will allow.

icon, an image. Contemporarily, refers to those symbols on a microcomputer screen which reference functions.

image area, the space on a printed piece within which art must be confined.

implied endorsement, promotional event in which marketer associates brand/service with another factor, the implication being that the factor has approved of the event even though manufacturer hasn't paid for the endorsement. Even a brand name of a store's *menu board* implies that the store management *endorses* the product.

impressions, the number of exposures of an advertisement to a defined group of persons.

imprint, using an existing printed piece, on which is printed additional *type*. Usually used to accommodate address or price changes.

impulse purchase, unplanned consumer purchase. Decision made at *point-of-sale*.

incentive, a motivational offering intended to secure extra effort on the part of a salesperson or purchase on the part of a consumer.

indicia, an imprinted designation on a mailing piece which indicates that postage, if used, has been prepaid. Eliminates need for individual envelope stamping.

infomercial, broadcast advertising designed to look like programming. Usually long, e.g.: 30 minutes, and run during off-peak hours when stations have programming voids and unsold airtime inventory. Often rates negotiated based upon sales response achieved. The print equivalent is called an *advertorial.*

in-house, any service that an agency provides using its own staff/facilities, as opposed to "farming out," or subcontracting the work.

insertion order, instructions from an advertiser allowing a publication to print an ad of a specific size, on a specific date, at an agreed upon rate.

instant coupon, *on-* or *in-packed coupons,* meant to be removed in-store and redeemed "on-the-spot."

instant winner, promotion technique in which participants know immediately whether or not they have won a prize.

institutional advertising, advertising designed to persuade readers/viewers of the merits of the corporation, as opposed to individual products/services. Often designed to encourage investment in the company's common stock.

interactive, buzzword for promotional techniques which permit consumer "interaction" with a marketer. Example: computerized *kiosk display* inviting shoppers to determine best form of product for them. Toll-free telephone lines, CD-ROM and PC-based on-line services are also *interactive* marketing.

internet, a vast network of computers that connects many of the world's businesses, institutions and individuals.

investment spending, expending marketing funds at a level that could not be justified by short-term sales volume. Usually done to get a business established, and achieve *break-even,* longer term or *pay-out.*

island display, a display of merchandise which stands alone in a store and can be shopped from 360°.

italic, in *type,* letterforms that slope to the right. If they slope to the left, they're called "backslant."

itinerant display, *point-of-sale* display which is moved from one retail outlet to another, on a scheduled basis, usually to amortize its expensive cost.

J

joint promotion, wherein two or more companies get together to promote brands, within a unified theme.

justify, to set *type* so that both left and right margins of all text lines are vertically aligned, giving a "squared-up" appearance because all lines are the same length. *Type* so set is said to be justified. Example: this book.

K

KISS, *acronymic* buzzword: "Keep It Simple, Stupid!"

keeper, *premium* offered to consumers in return for trying or inspecting a product, which is "yours to keep, even if you cancel (your subscription)" for example.

key account, major customer with high volume potential, usually handled by a senior sales representative.

kiosk, a free-standing, usually permanent, retail display. Might range from an interactive information center to an actual selling space.

knock-out, (*drop-out* or *reverse*), usually white lettering on a dark color background, created by the absence of ink on paper.

L

LED, (Light-Emitting Diode), crystalline semi-conducting device that glows red, especially used in electronic displays.

laminate, to apply a high-glass coating to enhance a printed piece and to provide protection from excessive handling.

laser printer, printing machine, usually associated with producing hard-copy computer output. Utilizes laser light to scan text/graphic images, transferring them to a photo-sensitive drum for printing.

laser printing, computer-peripheral printing, accomplished by a laser beam, toner, and fuser system.

layout, designer's conception of the finished job or the drawing of a proposed printed piece.

leave-behind, item, typically a *brochure* or *premium,* designed to be left with the prospect at the conclusion of a sales presentation.

letter press, the original method of mechanical printing, still widely-used, based on relief printing; i.e., ink is transferred from raised metal or rubber to the receiving surface.

life cycle, in marketing, the stages of a product's existence. Typically: Introduction > Growth > Maturation > Saturation > Decline.

lifestyle, buzzword referring to advertising which conveys a positive, "fun" image to people participating in everyday activities.

linage, in newspaper advertising, a measurement of the amount of advertising carried. Also, a reference to the size of an ad — a full-page ad is 2,400 lines, therefore a 600-line ad is 1/4 page.

line art, artwork with no tonal values, which can be directly reproduced without conversion to half-tone.

line conversion, photographic process that converts *continuous tone* art into *line art.*

list broker, company in the business of acquiring and renting mailing lists.

local rate, the price offered by regional media to local advertisers — usually lower than the rate charged to national advertisers.

logo, (logotype), corporate or brand name in specially-designed *typeface* or artistically rendered *typeface.*

loop, continuous piece of film or tape that replays without necessitating rewinding.

loss leader, product featured by retailer at below-cost pricing, in order to increase store traffic, to sell additional, profitable items.

lottery, illegal promotion which contain *chance, consideration* (i.e. purchase) and *prize.* A sweepstakes must eliminate consideration, a contest eliminates chance. States can legally conduct *lotteries.*

loyalty, measure of consumer commitment to a specific brand. Also, a type of promotion intended to foster consumer loyalty.

M

MBO, (Management By Objectives), style of business management that concentrates on 1) goals, 2) action plan, 3) periodic review, 4) appraisal.

magenta, a subtractive primary color, and one of the colors used in *four-color process.* Also called "red."

mail-in offer, promotion which requires consumers to respond by mail to receive an incentive. Often requires submission of *proofs-of-purchase.*

mail key, an identifying character-code, printed on a label or response/reply card, to enable a mail marketer to track performance of list selections or program alternatives.

makegood, advertisement run without charge, either because of reproduction, circulation shortfall or other error by the medium.

make-ready, to prepare press, and to adjust register-and-color on press to pre-determined specifications or to match proof before commencing production run.

margin, that part of the selling price of a product that remains after cost. Usually expressed in dollars/cents. If stated in percentage, it would be called profit.

markdown, the percentage of price reduction from "everyday" featured in a retailer's sale.

marketing, the combination of activities involved in the process of moving a product from its point of manufacture to its ultimate purchase by the consumer.

marketing mix, the combination of all elements utilized to market a product, including pricing, advertising, packaging, *promotion,* et al.

marketing plan, usually the annual document that sets *marketing* direction for a brand, and spells out the budgetary details for each element of the plan.

market potential, marketer's assessment of a product's ability or the ability of a given geographical area to deliver product sales.

market share, (share of market), percentage of a category sales accounted for by a brand. Expressed as either a percentage of units or dollars.

mark-up, the amount "added-on" to the cost, to get selling price. Expressed either in dollars or percent ($ mark-up ÷ $ cost = % mark-up). (See *profit.*)

masking, blocking out an unwanted portion of artwork, to prevent it from being reproduced.

mass display, large display of product in a retail store, usually in an *end-aisle* or *island* location, and in addition to normal shelf stock.

mass merchandiser, retail store selling various merchandise from a wide range of product categories; i.e., durable goods, clothing, drugs, entertainment, etc.

masthead, the displayed title of a journal that usually includes publishing, *editing*, location, and legal information.

matte, in *art*, a non-glossy finish. In printing, a varnish that gives a dull finish to the final production.

mature market, product category in which growth potential has peaked and volume has stabilized or is declining. Also: a reference to the "geriatric" or "senior citizen" market.

mechanical art, (reproduction art), *type* and *art* pasted on *board* along with color indications and other information which a printer requires for reproduction.

media, the means of communicating to consumers, whether print or electronic, mass or specialized.

media discounts, reductions from rate card, usually associated with some type of volume purchase.

media merchandising, promotional activity conducted by a medium, (for example, a radio station), on behalf of an advertiser's product/service. Usually as an extra, unmeasurable, "reason why" to persuade advertiser to utilize that medium. Activity can include on-air contests, press parties, et al.

medium, any vehicle used to convey an advertising message. Also: the type of tools/techniques used by an artist; e.g., *oil, acrylics,* and *photography* are "mediums."

merchandising, the marketing activities utilized to make a product available and visible at retail.

mix, in marketing the combination of elements in a marketing plan is called the "marketing mix."

mobile, *point-of-sale* signage designed to hang from store ceiling. Usually two-or-more parts, each hanging from another, which rotate in ambient air movement to attract attention.

mouse type, tiny, barely readable *type* that conveys a marketer's legal *copy*, usually on the back of a *coupon* or *sweepstakes* entry form.

multi-media, a presentation comprising two ore more *media*; i.e., 35mm slides, film and soundtrack.

N

900 number, a toll phone number used for promotional purposes, often to disseminate information or as a game or voting device. Caller pays toll.

national advertising, rate that local *media* charge national advertisers, generally **rate** is higher than the "local rate" that is offered to local customers.

negative, (film in reverse), printing film in negative form to make positive plates. Also: a *photostat* that has been reversed. (Black-to-white and white-to-black.)

neon, a *point-of-sale* sign utilizing glass tubing filled with gas which, when illuminated, produces brightly visible colorations.

niche marketing, buzzword for positioning brands to narrow target-audience segments.

Nielsen rating, a *media* rating measured and reported commercially, by the A.C. Nielsen company.

O

OSHA, (Occupational Safety and Health Administration), governmental agency charged with, among other things, worker safety. Impacts many promotion areas; e.g., shipping case specifications.

offset, a type of *lithography* utilizing a thin metal plate. The plate "offsets" its ink to a rubber roller, which in turn transfers the image to paper.

on-line, computer services which enable subscribers to access available data-bases, participate in typed conversations, and send/receive *E-mail* messages. Examples: Prodigy, CompuServ.

opaque, ink or material that is impermeable to light. Opposite of "transparent."

open-to-buy, buzzword referring to the situation when a *buyer* has been authorized to make purchase commitments.

opticals, film "tricks," created by a special editing camera, to product effects like *zooms*, enlargements, wipes, *dissolves*, spins, irises, etc.

outdoor, general term referring to *out-of-home media*, usually *billboards*, but including *transit*, *skywriting*, etc.

overlay, in *art*, any addition/variation to a *layout* which is "overlaid" onto a basic design.

overprint, the act of printing an additional message on a *pre-print*..

overrun, in print production, the quantity produced that exceeds the order quantity. Because of normal damage in the production process, a certain amount of *overrun* is necessary to achieve 100% of the ordered quantity.

oxymoron, Greek for "pointedly foolish." Refers to contradictory copy; e.g., "freezer burn," "jumbo shrimp," "same difference."

P

PERT, (Project Evaluation and Review Technique), a chronological flow chart detailing all decision-making phases of a project (by actual due dates), from initial planning through final implementation.

PI, (Per Inquiry), promotional advertising for which the *medium* is paid based upon number of persons who respond to the offering.

PIN, (Personal Identification Number), one uniquely assigned to an individual customer — a critical input to *interactive* marketing.

PM, (Push Money), *incentive* given to a distributor's salesperson to motivate him/her to *push* manufacturer's product in deference to others carried in his line.

PMAA, (Promotional Marketing Association of America), trade organization serving agencies and marketers in the promotion industry.

PMS, (Pantone Matching System), *trademark* of the most widely used color-matching system. Designed to enable artists/printers to specify and reproduce precise colors.

POPAI, (Point-of-Purchase Advertising Institute), trade organization serving producers and marketers involved with *point-of-sale* material.

POS, (Point-of-Sale), material, usually printed, that is designed to attract shopper attention, and stimulate a purchase, at the retail store. Also: *point-of-purchase*.

pallet display, an entire pallet-load of goods, packed together with *point-of-sale* material, intended to become a giant *display*, simply by fork-lifting into place and removing the protective wrapping.

pass-along, in *media*, a term used to describe the fact that a periodical may be read by several people, though only paid for one. Therefore, circulation + pass-along = total readership.

pastel, any color of a soft hue, light tint, pale.

paste-up, the act of producing *mechanical art..*

peel-off label, generally an adhesive label affixed to an adhesive backing. The resultant label can be adhered to a product or mailing piece, but the label itself can be removed without destroying the carrier.

pencil, term for a *rough* sketch of a promotion concept, often literally rendered with a pencil.

perfect bound, a book, magazine or pamphlet that is bound with glue, before cover is applied. The cover is then glued to the spine to form a permanent attachment of cover to text. As opposed to *saddle stitched*, spiral, sewn bindings, et al.

perforate, to cut/punch a line of small holes around a portion of printed material to facilitate the tearing out of that section.

performance allowance, allowance paid to retailer on a *bill-back* basis, only when that retailer has submitted proof of compliance with the terms of the *promotion*.

perishables, products with limited shelf life, as opposed to *durables*.

phantom shopper, undercover person who poses as a shopper, to test the acumen or performance of retail staff.

photo opportunity, in *public relations,* creating a situation of interest that will motivate press photographers to capture the scene for publication, on a non-paid basis.

piggy back, in advertising, a commercial that advertises two products of the same sponsor, usually on a back-to-back :30/:30 basis, for purchase efficiency.

poster, any large sign on paper or cloth, intended to attract consumer attention.

premium, merchandise offered either free or at a reduced price, to generate sales of a product at the consumer or manufacturer level.

premium rep, salesperson or manufacturer's representative who sells several lines of items to the promotion industry. Often has exclusivity in a geographic area.

pre-press, the critical operations which occur prior to a print run, including *layout, copy, photography, illustration, separating, stripping, assembly, proofing and plate-making*, et al.

pre-price, manufacturer marking/printing the retail price on a product package before delivering it to retail.

preprint, an advertisement printed by manufacturer, and sent to *medium* for insertion into periodical, often designed to accept additional localized or late-data, printing. Also: the advance printing of an advertisement prior to actual publication for publicity purposes.

price circle, that portion of *point-of-sale* signage that is reserved for the retailer to *imprint* or write in, pricing of the item in that store.

price point, pricing level that a marketer has determined will make a difference in consumer decisions. Example: 99¢ vs. $1.00.

prime time, in television, the evening hours characterized as heaviest viewing periods. For example, Monday-Saturday, 7-10:00 PM.

private label, *packaged goods* product, similar to a nationally advertised brand, but contract produced by retailer or wholesaler, and labeled accordingly.

process, type of printing that produces graduated tones by the use of dots, as opposed to flat images. (See *four-color process*.)

profit, the amount left after the cost is subtracted from the selling price. Expressed in either dollars or percent ($Profit ÷ $Sell Price = % Profit). Also: *margin* .

progs, (progressives), in *four-color process* printing; printed proofs showing the individual 4/colors separately as well as in combination. Specifically, *yellow + cyan, magenta, cyan* and black, showing the process effect of each color combination on the total job.

promotion, (sales promotion), marketing activities that support advertising or are used in lieu of it, to encourage purchase of product or service, and/or achieve retail availability/visibility of product.

promotion allowance, any of several types of *discounts* or *rebates* offered by a marketer to wholesalers, distributors or retailers in return for product featuring — usually in the form of distribution, display or advertised price feature.

proof, any of the several means of producing a trial impression of a print job, to check accuracy prior to the final press run.

proof of purchase, requirement by a marketer that must be remitted to qualify for his offering. Might be a *UPC symbol*, a unique portion of the package, a cash register tape or in some cases, all of the above.

proof seals, special insignias printed on a product package or added after the primary production process ("blown on"), which consumers can utilize as *proof -of-purchase*, for the purpose of claiming their *refund*.

publicity, tool of public relations. Generally nonpaid form of promotion involving obtaining editorial coverage which communicates product benefits or otherwise creates goodwill.

public service announcement, (PSA), an advertisement aired by a medium at no charge, because the content is in the public interest.

puffery, exaggerated claims in advertising which risk the perception of "unjustifiable."

pull, product movement generated by advertising and promotion which generates consumer demand. As opposed to *push* marketing activities.

push, a promotional approach opposite to *pull*, in which goods are loaded into the retail channel in the hope that they'll sell by virtue of display, price feature, etc.

Q

quantity discount, manufacturer's discount to the trade, tied to greater quantity purchases of manufacturer's product.

R

RAB, (Radio Advertising Bureau), association that promotes the use of radio as an advertising medium. (800) 232-3131.

ROI, (Return on Investment), measurement of the success of a marketing program calculated by comparing the revenue generated to the amount invested in the campaign.

ROP, (Run Of Press), advertising, generally refers to newspaper, where advertiser has no control over the position (location) of the ad in that paper. Publisher's discretion prevails.

RSC, (Regular Slotted Carton), shipping carton, usually *corrugated*, that folds up and around the object to be packed. Slots create flaps which fold over, forming a secure package.

rating, in electronic *media*, a statement of the percentage of homes with radios or TVs listening to or watching, a particular program.

readership, a measurement of the total number of persons to read a periodical, including base circulation, plus *pass-along*.

rebate, an incentive to purchase in the form of a discount mailed to consumers after their purchase. Usually refers to high-ticket items (appliances, cars), as opposed to package goods, where the term *refund* is more common.

recall, (See *awareness*.) the act of a marketer requesting retailers to return goods, for full credit, which have been determined defective.

redeem, (redemption), in consumer terms, to turn in *coupons* for their face value or trading stamps of their *premium* value. In trade terms, to accept those *coupons* or trading stamps.

refund, monetary reward to consumer, in return for *proof-of-purchase* . Usually delivered by "refund certificate" and redeemed by mail. Differs from a *coupon*, which is store-redeemed, and a *rebate*, which is usually associated with higher-ticket items; e.g., appliances.

register, in printing, the correct positioning of each color run so that the result is "in register."

registry mark, the indication "®" which signifies that a word/logo is a "registered" *trademark*. Also, in *paste-up*, marks placed on base art and on *overlays* to insure perfect alignment of multiple images. Usually crosses in circles.

release, in *public relations*, a story or item sent to the press. Also, in photography, a legal statement authorizing the use of a performer's image by the marketer in advertising.

re-run, in printing, to redo a job because the initial quality was unacceptable. In television, the airing of previously-used programming.

residual, payment to talent featured in broadcast commercials on a "per-use" basis.

retailer, an operator who sells products to the ultimate *consumer* by means of a store which stocks product. Usually offers no exclusivity to manufacturers, as opposed to a *dealer,* which typically refers to a retailer who carries a limited number of lines.

rough, loose drawing of the proposed promotion concept. (See pencil, thumbnail.)

rough-cut, in video, the first edit of film scenes. In *point-of-sale,* the first "hand-cut" prototype of a display piece.

rub-off, a promotion technique in which a hidden message is covered with a special ink that can be rubbed off by the consumer to unveil the message. Most often used in *instant win* sweepstakes.

S

SKU, (Stock-Keeping Unit), term to describe the various different packagings of a brand. Every size, flavor, put-up, et al., is one "stock-keeping unit." Usually also the number of line entries a retailer must put on his inventory computer.

SPA, (Sales Promotion Allowance or Special Purchase Allowance), discount incentive offered to trade during a specified time period, usually to support a promotional event.

SRDS, (Standard Rate & Data Service), major firm in the field of reporting *media* rates, circulation, and other marketing information. (212) 702-6885.

saddle stitch, binding method where wire *stitches* (staples) are located in the back fold of brochures, pamphlets, etc. Best limited to 80 pages, but is determined by the bulk of paper stock used.

salable sample, small, trial size of a package goods product that is offered to retailers to sell, usually at a very low price, to obtain consumer trial. Less expensive and more controllable than free sampling, but more limited in reach.

sales aids, collateral material designed to help the salesperson do his/her job. Includes *brochures, flip charts, giveaways,* et al.

sales incentive, a reward, usually in the form of cash or product, for member(s) of sales staff who exceed selling quota. Often part of a program designed to create ambition within the sales force, by make them aware of reward benefits for excellent performance.

sampling, marketer's technique of achieving trial by getting product into hands of consumers, usually free, but often at a reduced cost; i.e., *trial size* or *salable sample.*

sans serif, a *font* or *typeface* where the design doesn't incorporate finishing-off strokes; e.g., "**H**" as opposed to "**H**." Also known as *gothic* type.

scanner, electronic device used at checkout to "read" *UPC* symbols and automatically record the transaction. Also: pre-programmed computerized *color separation* camera using high-intensity light or *laser* light, to scan the original.

SciTex, brand name for a highly-sophisticated color separation computer. A similar computer is *Chromacom.*

score, in print production, a "blind" depressed rule in paper, creating a natural fold to make folding easier.

screen, a field of *dots,* recreating a continuous tone image for printing.

screen printing, method of printing where ink is forced through a stenciled cloth "screen," one color at a time. Generally for low-quantity production runs.

seamless, large roll of paper used by photographers to create a background with no "horizon" line.

self-liquidator, *premium* offered to consumers at a price which totally covers the marketer's cost of buying and fulfilling the offer.

self-mailer, *direct mail* piece designed so that it can be mailed without envelope or outside packaging.

sell sheet, promotional/program information distributed to product sales representatives, which is specifically designed to provide sales motivation/assistance.

serif, in *type*, a short line projecting from the top or bottom of the main stroke of a letter. "H" has serifs. Conversely, "H" is *sans serif*.

sheet-fed, any printing press that accepts paper pre-cut into sheets, as opposed to rolls (*webs*) of paper.

shelf talker, *point-of-sale* signage designed to snap into the retailers *price channel*.

Sherman Antitrust Law, Federal law prohibiting elimination of competition in a specific industry. Essentially makes the creation of monopolies illegal.

shipper, the outer container, typically an *RSC*, in which package goods product is shipped. Usually the minimum quantity available.

show card, style of hand-lettering used by sign makers.

showcase, to present a product in a unique environment, and to it's best advantage. Also: an enclosed, often locked, permanent display.

shrinkage, trade lingo for the amount of merchandise received but not sold, either due to shoplifting or employee theft.

shrink wrap, wrap which bundles product together tightly/neatly for better handling/shipping.

side-stitched, (stabbed), binding method in which loose leaves are stapled together, usually at the left-hand edge.

signature, (See *form*), in printing, the number of pages on one *form*, when folded and trimmed, make up a part of the finished book. When finished, all signatures are gathered in sequence and bound.

silhouette, in *art*, to separate an image from its background so that it can stand alone or be superimposed against a new background.

silkscreen, a specialized *flat color* printing process useful for short runs, where vibrant colors are required.

slotting allowances, an incentive paid to a retailer in return for each "slot," or space, granted on that retailer's shelf or fixture.

small-space advertising, periodical advertisements, placed in units that comprise fractions of a page.

snipe, a small printed patch or *banner*, applied to the face of a display to change information. Also, a blank adhesive-backed patch to cover information not applicable.

software, programming stored on hard or floppy disks, which is necessary to drive computer *hardware*; i.e., printer or computer.

space, generally the portion of print *media* devoted to accepting advertising.

spec, (speculation), work done without advance fee in hopes that client will like it and ultimately pay for it.

specifications (specs), a statement of the requirements of a production job ranging from paper weight, to printing technique, to number of illustrations, et al., including *bindery* operations.

spiff, trade nickname for *sales incentive.* (See *PM.*)

split run, two different ad or promotional messages run in the same *medium*, usually to test the effectiveness or *pull,* of one message versus the other.

spot, buzzword for broadcast time slot devoted to a commercial. Also: the buying of broadcast time on a local market basis, as opposed to national network buying.

stat, *(photostat),* photo print of *art* made by a camera. Usually black on white photographic paper.

stencil, rudimentary printing technique, in which ink is applied through holes cut into a sheet.

stock, any element, photography, illustration, molds, paper, etc., that already exists in available inventory for a marketer's use.

stock paper, popular printing papers that are made available on a regular basis in pre-determined sizes and continually available in quantity from merchants.

stock photo, an existing picture, usually a *transparency*, available for use in an ad by buying the right to use it from a "*stock* house."

store check, usually the act of home-office people or their designees , visiting retail stores to gather *marketing* intelligence.

storyboard, presentation of a proposed video or commercial, using rough illustrations adjacent to script, as indication of final film.

strategy, steps recommended as necessary to achieve an *objective.*

stripping, (See *film* and *pre-press*), attaching, putting together, assembling in *negative* film form the separate elements of an ad, *brochure, flyer* or other printed materials into one cohesive unit.

stuffer, printed literature intended for insertion into a mailing envelope. Usually refers to extra literature, which subject matter is extraneous to the main purpose of the mailing.

style book, a collection of specifications compiled by a marketer to ensure that suppliers make consistent and proper use of *logos, colors, typography,* et al.

subhead, important text on a *layout* that is subordinate or secondary in importance, to the main *headline.*

super, *type* message which appears over a video picture, usually via double exposure or "fading" together of two camera shots.

sweepstakes, a *promotion* which requires only chance to win, and therefore: 1) no purchase (*consideration*) can be required; and 2) winner(s) can be determined by random drawing. (See lottery.)

synergism, *marketing* buzzword which suggests that two elements of a program combined provide greater impact than the sum total of each of them separately.

T

TPR, acronym for Temporary Price Reduction, a type of *allowance*.

TVB, (Television Bureau of Advertising), association that promotes the use of television as an advertising medium. (212) 486-1111

table tent, *point of sale* signage intended to sit on a restaurant table or bar-top. Usually a simple folded device in the shape of a tent.

tag, An additional message at the end of an electronic *media* advertisement.

tearsheet, advertisement printed by a periodical, and set to the client, unbound, as a proof or sample. Historically, these ads were literally "torn" from finished magazines.

teaser, *copy* intended to get reader to "turn page" or "look inside." Also, a mailing sent in advance of a major mailing to arouse consumer interest in the mail to follow.

telemarketing, selling, soliciting or researching via telephone.

test market, defined marketing area in which an alternative *marketing mix* can be evaluated versus the national plan or a new product introduction marketing mix evaluated.

text, the output of a typesetter, the words that go on a *layout*. Also: *body copy*.

thumbnail, small sketch which gives *rough* idea of the position and elements of a design

tie-in promotion, (group promotion), event that involves two or more brands, with a consumer incentive to purchase both.

touchy-feeley, slang for a promotional technique which enables prospects to physically "play" with the product.

trade advertising, advertising intended not for consumers but for the various factors who influence consumer availability; i.e., *wholesalers, retailers, reps, salespeople, etc.*

trademark, the mark of a product/brand claimed as owned by a marketer; often marked as ™ if mark has been applied for, ® if it has been registered.

trade promotion, (trade deal), incentives given/paid to trade factors to motivate *stocking, display, feature* of a marketer's product (s).

trade show, exhibition conducted for members of a specific industry.

traffic builder, any promotional activity that generates additional store visitations by shoppers.

trim size, finished size of a printed piece after waste is trimmed away.

truckload allowance, trade *incentive* based upon a marketer passing along savings realized by shipping a full truck to a single destination.

turnkey, in *promotion*, a packaged event, including all materials required so that a *wholesaler* or *retailer* can field the promotion by himself.

turnover, the number of times a product's average retail inventory is moved (sold) during a year.

twin pack, special pack of product, where two packages are banded together and sold at a special price.

two-color printing, reproduction utilizing two colors of ink, one of which is usually black, to produce an image less expensively than *4-color process*, but more visually arresting than "black & white" printing.

two-fer, promotion offer of "two for price of one," commonly associated with theatrical event tickets.

typeface, general term used to describe the styles of lettering available in *typesetting*. The five general classes of typeface: *roman; italic; script; gothic;* and *text.*

typeset, to create *type* of a quality usable for reproduction, whether electronically or mechanically.

typo, abbreviation for "typographical error" within a *text* block.

U

UPC, (Universal Product Code), packaging symbol, consisting of numbers and a series of bar stripes, which can be read by *check-out scanners*. The UPC automatically registers brand name, flavor, size, price, and inventory information.

USP, (Unique Selling Proposition), *marketing* buzzword used, and made famous by Rosser Reeves. A concept that advertising should seek to give a product a unique identity or capitalize on one it inherently has.

umbrella, buzzword for a theme which encompasses a multi-level series of promotional activities.

undeliverables, mailing pieces that cannot be delivered, usually because of incorrect address or name not resident at that address.

unduplicated audience, maximum number of prospects reached by a mailing/advertisement. *Households* receiving two mailings are counted as one "unduplicated" *HH.*

upper case, in *type*, the capital letters of a *typeface.*

V

VO, (voiceover), in video, a voice of actor on soundtrack but not seen in film. An "Off-Stage Announcer."

value-added, term to describe any promotional technique perceived by the consumer to add value to the product, therefore not risking a negative image connotation as might occur with mere price-cutting.

visual aid, any "sight-oriented" device utilized to "add interest" to a presentation.

voluntary chain, group of independent stores who operate as a buying unit, to achieve volume discounts and merchandising opportunities. Usually organized and sponsored by a *wholesaler*, and often operating under a group trade name.

W

WATS, (Wide-Area Telephone Service), a trademark (AT&T) of a phone system which offers subscribers unlimited use for a flat monthly charge. Usually associated with 800-*numbers.*

WYSIWYG, (What You See Is What You Get), in *electronic imaging*, a feature that enables all elements of a project to be previewed on the CRT monitor, prior to print-out.

watermark, design pressed into paper during the production process, which identifies its manufacturer. Usually perceived as a statement of quality.

wearables, term generally referred to *brand ID* merchandise intended to be worn; i.e., T-shirts, caps, et. al.

web offset, type of *offset* printing in which paper is fed from large rolls, as opposed to *sheet-fed*. Usually used in large *press-runs*.

wholesaler, a company in the business of buying, warehousing, selling to *retailers*, shipping and invoicing a manufacturer's products. Offers no exclusivity, as opposed to a *distributor*, which generally refers to a wholesaler who carries non-competing lines.

widow, single word at the end of a paragraph, left on a line of its own. Usually considered bad form, which should be corrected by editing.

window banner, *point-of-sale* signage intended to be hung in a retailer's window.

window envelope, envelope which needs no label, because the name/address on the inserted letter can be seen through a cellophane panel.

work-in-progress, promotion agency billing term, wherein partial invoices are submitted prior to a production job being completed, to cover vendor and/or labor costs incurred.

X - Y

xerography, the formation of pictures or copies of graphic materials, by the action of light on an electrically charged surface in which the image is usually developed with powders. A generic process, but predominantly associated with the Xerox Corporation.

Z

zap, buzzword, indicating the capability of a consumer, armed with a remote control device to switch channels and avoid commercials.

zip+4 code, latest version of the USPS "Zoning Improvement Plan." The standard 5-digit ZIP is followed by 4 more, 2 of which define a USPS sector, and 2 others a segment within that sector.

Zip-a-tone, trademark (Zipatone, Hillside IL) for a material used to add shading to artwork, consisting of various tones printed on plastic rub-down material.

zoom, to use a lens to enlarge/reduce *art* image. Also: in filming, a fast, continuous camera move in on or away from, a given subject.

Special Thanks to . . .

A sincere "Thank You" to these members of the advertising community for their support in making this book possible. Their "Permission to publish . . ." allowed the author to showcase the finest examples of desktop publishing ever assembled in one textbook. (To help you in your advertising role.) Participants include:

- American Institute of Small Business (p. 147)
- American Seminars Leaders Association (p. 148)
- Bachman's (pp. 116, 141)
- Braemar Mailing Service (p. 144)
- Bruegger's Bagels (pp. 43, 150)
- Byerly's (p. 149)
- Caribou Coffee (p. 141)
- Collins Outdoor Advertising (p. 118)
- Cub Foods (pp. 51, 88)
- Emma Krumbee's (p. 129)
- Empire Diamond (p. 57)
- Farm-Oyl Company (pp. 9, 23, 133, 155)
- M.A. Gedney Company (pp. 51, 85)
- Hirshfield's (p. 17, 64)
- Jamestown Color Lab (p. 57)
- Kinko's (p. 178)
- Land O' Lakes, Inc./Campbell Mithun Esty (pp. 167-169)
- Larson Storm Doors (pp. 46, 47, 101-103)
- Lyndale Hardware (p. 123)
- McGraw Hill (p. 109)
- Midway Container (p. 143)
- Midway Master Distributing (p. 111)
- Minnesota Forest Industries/ Colle McVoy (p. 45)
- Nate's Clothing/Jim Kosmas & Associates (p. 115)
- National Fluid Milk Processor Promotion Board (p. 153)
- Nelson Agri-Center (pp. 117, 118, 126)

- Old Home Foods, Inc. (p. 87)
- Park Upholstery/Gordon Robinson & Associates (pp. 14, 61)
- Penn Cycle (pp. 5, 125)
- St. Catherine's College (p. 44)
- Sawhorse Designers & Builders (p. 163)
- Scotts Company (p. 99)
- Sedgwick Heating/Contractors Success Group (p. 96)
- Sela Roofing & Remodeling (p. 90)
- TCF Bank (pp. 42, 160)
- 3M Company (p. 141)
- Toro Company (p. 106)
- Travel Michigan (p. 55)
- Twin City Radiator (p. 57)
- University of Minnesota (pp. 86, 188)
- Wave Car Wash (p. 140)
- WCCO Radio (p. 83)
- Wild Bird Store (pp. 41, 134)
- Ziegler-Cat/Gordon Robinson & Associates (p. 112)

Thanks, also to . . .
- Adams Media Corporation
- Carol Publishing Group
- Al Hietala
- High Yield Management
- Icon Productions
- Dave Lee
- Ray Mithun
- Robert Pile
- Promotional Products Association International
- Westco Recognition Advertising